MW00596510

Latin Laughs:

A Production of Plautus' *Poenulus*

◆ Student Edition ◆

by

John H. Starks, Jr.

Matthew D. Panciera

Christopher Brunelle

David M. Johnson

Serena Zabin

Elizabeth Reynolds

Beth Calamia

Bolchazy–Carducci Publishers, Inc.
Wauconda, Illinois

Contributing Editor:
Gaby Huebner

General Editor:
Laurie K. Haight

Cover Illustration:
Comic Mask

Cover Design:
Bensen Studios

Book Design and Typography:
Kay McGinnis Ritter

©1997 Bolchazy-Carducci Publishers, Inc.

Bolchazy-Carducci Publishers, Inc.
1000 Brown Street
Wauconda, Illinois 60084

Printed in the United States of America
1997

ISBN 0-86516-323-5

Library of Congress Cataloging-in-Publication Data

Plautus, Titus Maccius
   [Poenulus]
   Latin Laughs: a production of Plautus' Poenulus / by John H.
Starks, Jr. . . . [et al.]. -- Student ed.
     p. cm.
   "Latin text with grammatical commentary and running vocabulary of
a 1994 production of Plautus' comedy, Poenulus"--Publisher's info.
   ISBN 0-86516-323-5 (alk. paper)
   1. Latin drama (Comedy)--Problems, exercises, etc.   I. Starks,
John H., 1966-   . II. Title.
PA6568.P7 1997
872'.01--dc21
                                                97-8784
                                                CIP

Preface

Latin Laughs is a complete comedy kit centered around a production of Plautus' *Poenulus* put on by the University of North Carolina-Chapel Hill Classics Department in the spring of 1994. Much time and effort has gone into writing and gathering this material by a dedicated group of graduate students at UNC who hope that this will provide a convenient and entertaining supplement to your Latin instruction.

Your student edition of this booklet contains our edited text of Plautus' *Poenulus* (about three-fifths of its original length), a facing page grammar- and content-focused commentary, and a complete glossary of every word in the play.

We edited Plautus' text in order to make the play of suitable length for a live modern audience, and also to allow ample time for English explication of the plot during the live performance of the play. Condensed versions of these English descriptions of the major events and attitudes expressed in the play can be found at the beginning of each scene. Our cuts from Plautus' original text are only noted by the listing of the original line numbers for Plautus' scenes at the beginning of each of our edited scenes. Our additions to and adaptations from Plautus' text are noted in the accompanying commentary or in the director's notes (found in the Teacher Edition of this book). Many of the most difficult archaisms common in Plautus have been converted into their more familiar classical Latin forms or are explained in notes.

Our grammatical commentary is geared toward you, the student of Latin, but is focused on helping you understand the Latin rather than giving you too many lines translated outright. The commentary also contains valuable information on ancient history, society, and comedy so that you can enjoy the most important aspect of Roman comedy, its humor.

The live, dramatic quality of Plautus should help you see that Latin was a lively language used primarily for oral (not written or read) communication, as are most languages. Plautus will give you the best possible examples of everyday Latin conversation on subjects like food, the weather, love, and, best of all, jokes.

The glossary was also written with you, the student, in mind. We have included in it every word from our edited version of Plautus' *Poenulus*. So unlike many other Latin texts you will use, this one has all the vocabulary, grammar, and text right there for you.

The Teacher Edition contains a set of director's notes that explain our videotape interpretations of the play, some supplementary information about Roman comedy and the theater, oral Latin exercises derived from this text, and a modern translation of the text. You may ask your teacher about any of these items that might help you better understand Plautus.

Finally, there is the videotape. The video presents a LIVE stage performance of the *Poenulus*. The tape features English plot explication before the first, third, and fifth "acts" of the edited play. Our plot explicator is a modern equivalent of the Roman *prologus* who seeks to keep everybody up to date on what's going to happen in the next act, while also teaching some valuable and crucial Latin words and phrases that are used frequently throughout the play. This also helps to break the pure Latin text into three segments that last about twenty minutes each. Act and Scene numbers from the original Latin play appear at the bottom of the screen throughout the given scene. A visual *Dramatis Personae* is also provided at the opening of the play so that you can talk about the individual characters before the play and recognize them right away.

Remember that live stage performances have different light and sound quality from "Made for TV" productions. Ours was a polished production of Plautus, but not a professional one. We have found that the videotape, despite its rough exterior, is an excellent tool for bringing live Latin text and visual images of ancient culture into the classroom.

This booklet and videotape began as an educational project called *Latin Live: Plautus' Poenulus in Production*. Our focus was to reach out to the North Carolina community of Latin secondary programs with a presentation that would show how fun and interesting Latin can be when presented in living drama and language. We informed every North Carolina Latin teacher we could identify and invited all comers from the university community to see our Latin play, which we had rehearsed over a gruelling three-month period. With the help of a great cast and crew, the result was a huge success, packing the house with a total of more than one thousand spectators for three live shows, delivered primarily in Latin. Who says Latin is a dead language?

As director, I would like to thank several institutions and individuals that made this whole project possible: The North Carolina Humanities Council, Classical Association of the Middle West and South, and The North Carolina Classical Association, as well as more than sixty donors who helped us with the original costs of production. A very special thank you to our staff of actors and crew who made the whole project a great success. You will find their names on the following pages and at the end of the videotape. Finally, I thank those who put the most time into the creation of this packet, The Instructional Packet Committee for *Latin Live: Plautus' Poenulus in Production* – Matthew D. Panciera, Christopher Brunelle, and Dave Johnson, the three who wrote and designed the commentary, glossary, and translation – and Serena Zabin, Elizabeth Reynolds, and Beth Calamia, who contributed exercises and cultural material. Thanks also to Ladislaus Bolchazy, Laurie Haight, and Gaby Huebner of Bolchazy-Carducci, and to our compositor and page designer, Kay McGinnis Ritter, for helping us in so many ways to polish, professionalize, and distribute these materials to more teachers. For the committee and myself, I wish you the best in your use of these tools.

We would appreciate any feedback you can give us on how you used these materials so that we may learn more from this whole process of educational writing and project development. You can contact any of us through the Department of Classics at UNC-Chapel Hill, CB #3145, 212 Murphey Hall, Chapel Hill NC 27599-3145.

John H. Starks, Jr.
Chapel Hill, NC

Contents

The Theater of Marcellus at Rome
From: M. Bieber: *The History of the Greek and Roman Theater*
Princeton 1961, illu. 643.

Introduction

The *Poenulus* is not often performed, but then neither are many other Latin comedies. This play has been condemned for its double plot, its length, and its humor, but (as we discovered, especially in putting the *Poenulus* on stage) it is a funny play with much to commend it.

The *Poenulus* was probably written sometime during the decade and a half after the Second Punic War. Today it is usually only recognized by scholars for its Prologue and its "Punic" text. Plautus' Prologue (not included in our edited text, but integrated into the text of our *Prologus* on the videotape) is a very interesting commentary on the republican theater. As for the "Punic" recorded in the manuscripts of Plautus' *Poenulus*, see my remarks throughout the commentary on scenes 5.1 and 5.2 and the special introductory Director's Note for Act 5 in the Teacher Edition, as well as the Appendix to this book containing the original "Punic" lines and our adaptations.

What stands out about the *Poenulus* from my director's standpoint is not the "weakness" of its web of two plots to trick the pimp, but the infinite variety of characters that cross the stage and help to paint a picture of the entire Plautine comedic world. This play contains most of the classic stock characters (see Some Cultural Aspects of the *Poenulus* in the Teacher Edition) blended together into a nice mix of different comic potentials. We have a bonus in the *senex* role, for here it is a foreigner, a Carthaginian, who allows for great costuming and humorous confusions of language and culture. The villain is a pimp, despised as all comic pimps are, not so much for the immoral nature of their profession as for their tendency to be greedy and cheat people out of their money. The *adulescens* is a typical young man in love with a prostitute he can't have and in possession of a slave he can't control, but whom he uses for subterfuge when it benefits him. There are two sisters of a very different stripe, but both are prostitute slaves trapped in the world of the pimp. We have the typical bragging soldier, a very blustery and angry fellow full of himself. There is a unique chorus of three mooching professional witnesses who are a key to the comedy of this play, though they present some problems with the plot's flow. The slaves include the wily *servus callidus* Milphio who is the agent of the plot, the grumpy eunuch Syncerastus, and the *vilica/pseudo-miles* Collybisca.

The chance to present on stage a culture as interesting and as important to the ancient world as that of the Carthaginians was also an important element in my choice of this play. Here we can teach several important points about a people that brought Rome almost as low as it ever had been or ever would be. Roman stereotypes of Carthaginians fill Act 5 of this play, but considering the destruction Carthage had brought on Italy not long before the *Poenulus*' composition, Plautus' treatment is remarkably balanced. Plautus avoids the easy option of making the Carthaginian the villain, and rather gives the kindly Carthaginian a good ribbing, but then rewards him with the starring role. This play becomes one long vehicle of fun leading to the presentation of this likable foreigner.

I warn you too that in my production of this play I have taken the approach that anachronistic props and jokes help make Latin lots of fun and that overacting with lots of movement is key to keeping audience interest. I believe in a live stage, not static speechmakers. We hope that you will enjoy the play as Latin and as comedy.

We proudly offer you our version of Plautus' *Poenulus*, or "The Puny Punic."

John H. Starks, Jr.
Director of Latin Live

The Theater of Pompeius at Rome
Reconstruction (Canina)
from: J.A. Hanson: *Roman Theater-Temples*, Princeton 1959, illu. 17.

Poenulus

T. MACCI PLAUTI

Edited Text and Commentary

Dramatis Personae
for Plautus' *Poenulus*
(as performed on the videotape and with abbreviations as used in the text)

Prologus   Cecil W. Wooten
  a plot explicator and narrator on videotape

Agorastocles adulescens (AG.)   Christopher Brunelle
  a lovesick young man

Milphio servus (MI.)   Matthew D. Panciera
  a sly slave of Agorastocles

Adelphasium meretrix (ADE.)   Liza Reynolds
  a prostitute slave of Lycus and Agorastocles' love interest

Anterastilis meretrix (ANTE.)   Rebecca Benefiel
  another prostitute and Adelphasium's sister

Ancilla   Cynthia Glidden
  a slave attendant to the two sisters

Lycus leno (LY.)   David Johnson
  the villain, a slimy pimp who owns the sisters

Antamoenides miles (ANTA.)   Ed Heil
  a soldier, customer of Lycus

Advocati (ADV.)   Beth Calamia, Brian Lund, D. Hunt
  a chorus of three slow, parasitic, professional witnesses

Collybisca vilica (CO.)   Alice Ann Moore
  Agorastocles' female country estate manager and ersatz soldier

Syncerastus servus (SY.)   Amy Jones
  a grumpy eunuch, Lycus' slave

Hanno Poenus (HA.)   Christopher McDonough
  a Carthaginian searching for his kidnapped daughters

Giddenis nutrix (GI.)   Cynthia Glidden
  Lycus' slave, nurse to the two sisters

Pueri   Brian Lund, Amy Jones
  two Carthaginian bearers, attendants to Hanno

Praeco   Mark Beck
  the bouncer who gets rid of rowdies and doubles as Agorastocles' tough

1.1

9 **istuc:** an alternative form of *istud.*

ausim: Agorastocles uses the subjunctive (perfect tense, from *audeo*) to express his mock scorn and disbelief at Milphio's previous line: "Would I dare…?!?"

10 **quin:** "indeed," "in fact."

11 **mihi:** is governed by *dolet* from the previous line.

13 **istuc:** refers to Agorastocles' last line, "*amo immodeste.*"

14 **dico:** *dico, dicere* "to mean," "to refer to."

15 **maiusculam:** from *maior, maius* ("greater," "older") and the diminutive *-culus, -a, -um;* thus, "a little bit older." Agorastocles' love, Adelphasium, is his next-door neighbor (her master the pimp lives next door), and has a younger sister Anterastilis, thus Agorastocles' need to define which of the two sisters he loves. This is plot explication for the audience's benefit, as Milphio tells us he has heard this all before (line 16).

18 **illius:** Adelphasium.

lutumst: = *lutum est.*

lutulentius: "filthier."

19 **vin:** = *visne.*

nequam dare: "to make trouble" for someone (in the dative case), "to play a trick" on someone (in the dative case).

em: an interjection. "Here you are," or "Take this," or "How about this?"

dato: future imperative of *do, dare.*

20 **dierectus:** a word of uncertain meaning, used when one person dismisses another.

vero serio: "seriously."

22 **iocare:** = *iocaris.*

24 **tibi:** dative of possession: "Are there gold coins **to you**?" or in better English, "Do you have gold coins?"

intus: "inside" (i.e., Agorastocles' house).

---

¹*We had to cut a good number of whole lines, and parts of others, to make the play short enough to be performed in one evening. We provide line numbers from the original text (as printed in the Oxford Classical Text) at the beginning of each scene.*

1.1 [original lines 129–209, with cuts]¹

Agorastocles declares to his slave Milphio his love for the girl next door. The only problem is that the girl, Adelphasium, is a prostitute, owned by the pimp Lycus, and it would take a great deal of money to buy her freedom. Milphio devises a complicated scheme to trick the pimp: they will disguise Agorastocles' slave Collybisca as a soldier come to town for a good time. When Lycus takes her (and her money) into his house to entertain her, he will be guilty of theft of Agorastocles' property and the young man will be awarded all the pimp's possessions (including Adelphasium) in court. They begin to put their plan into motion when Adelphasium and her sister, Anterastilis, come out of the pimp's house.

AGORASTOCLES. Saepe ego res multas tibi mandavi, Milphio,

dubias, egenas, inopiosas consili,

quas tu sapienter, docte et cordate et cate

mihi reddidisti opiparas opera tua.

5   quibus pro bene factis fateor deberi tibi

et libertatem et multas gratas gratias.

MILPHIO. Nunc mihi blandidicus es: heri in tergo meo

tris facile corios contrivisti bubulos.

AG. Egone istuc ausim facere, praesertim tibi?

10   quin si feriri video te, extemplo dolet.

MI. Mihi quidem hercle. AG. Immo mihi. MI. Istuc mavelim.

sed quid nunc tibi vis? AG. Cur ego apud te mentiar?

amo immodeste. MI. Meae istuc scapulae sentiunt.

AG. At ego hanc vicinam dico Adelphasium meam,

15   lenonis huius meretricem maiusculam.

MI. Iam pridem equidem istuc ex te audivi. AG. Differor

cupidine eius. sed lenone istoc Lyco,

illius domino, non lutumst lutulentius.

MI. Vin tu illi nequam dare nunc? AG. Cupio. MI. Em me dato.

20   AG. Abi dierectus. MI. Dic mihi vero serio:

vin dare malum illi? AG. Cupio. MI. Em eundem me dato.

AG. Iocare. MI. Vin tu illam hodie sine dispendio

tuo tuam libertam facere? AG. Cupio, Milphio.

MI. Ego faciam ut facias. sunt tibi intus aurei

25 **eis:** "the gold coins."

Philippi: The *Philippus* was a gold coin of King Philip II of Macedon (who reigned 359–336 B.C.), father of Alexander the Great. In Plautus' Calydon, this coin would represent the ultimate in hard currency. Three hundred of these would be a ridiculously huge amount of gold to be sitting around Agorastocles' house.

27 **dono:** "for a gift," "as a gift."

qui: not the nominative of *qui, quae, quod,* but an adverb: "How?"

28 **Collybisca…Collybiscus:** Milphio suddenly hits upon the strategy to disguise Collybisca as a male farm manager so that the pimp will not realize she works for Agorastocles. He quickly changes *vilica* "female country estate manager" to *vilicus* "male country estate manager." This was not part of Plautus' *Poenulus,* but our own adaptation. For further explanation see the director's note on this line.

urbest: = *urbe est.*

29 **satin:** = *satis·ne.*

30 **quo:** "to where?"

33 Remember that the indirect statement introduced by *dicat* continues in this line.

36 **rogato:** future imperative of the verb *rogo, rogare.*

veneritne: perfect subjunctive in an indirect question.

37 **continuo:** "immediately."

38 **quin:** When preceded by a phrase that indicates a lack of doubt (Milphio's question assumes Agorastocles is not in doubt), *quin* means "that."

39–42 Milphio's plans to trick Lycus the pimp into thinking that Collybisca, who actually is a slave and belongs to Agorastocles, is a free person. Then, when Lycus invites Collybisca into his house, he will have stolen Agorastocles' property, slave, and money. The name Collybisca is related to the Greek word for "money bag," which is appropriate since she will be the one to carry Agorastocles' money into the pimp's house. When Lycus is caught, Agorastocles will be able to bring him before the praetor and be awarded his entire household (including Adelphasium).

42 **fovea:** *fovea, -ae,* f., "pit," "trap."

44 **Aphrodisia:** a festival in honor of Aphrodite, Greek goddess of love, and therefore patron of pimps and prostitutes.

47 **ut ferat fallaciam:** "how to pull off this deception."

51 **cui:** The antecedent of this relative pronoun is the pimp, and it is in the dative case because he is the person "at whom" the catapult is aimed.

ballistast: = *ballista est.*

52 **hau multo post:** "not long after," "soon."

53 **eccam:** "Look!" or "Here she is!"

25 trecenti nummi Philippi? **AG.** Quid eis facturus es? **MI.** Tace.

totum lenonem tibi cum tota familia

dabo hodie dono. **AG.** Qui id facturus es? **MI.** Iam scies.

tua Collybisca … Collybisc*us*! … nunc in urbest vilica … vilic*us*;

eam hic non novit leno. satin intellegis?

30 **AG.** Intellego hercle, sed quo evadas nescio.

MI. Ei dabitur aurum, ut ad lenonem deferat

dicatque se peregrinum esse ex alio oppido:

se amare velle atque obsequi animo suo;

leno ad se accipiet auri cupidus ilico:

35 celabit hominem et aurum. **AG.** Consilium placet.

MI. Rogato servus veneritne ad eum tuus.

ille me censebit quaeri: continuo tibi

negabit. quid tu dubitas quin extempulo

dupli tibi, auri et hominis, fur leno sit?

40 neque id unde efficiat habet: ubi in ius venerit,

addicet praetor familiam totam tibi.

ita decipiemus fovea lenonem Lycum.

AG. Ego in aedem Veneris eo, nisi quid vis, Milphio.

Aphrodisia hodie sunt. **MI.** Scio. **AG.** Oculos volo

45 meos delectare munditiis meretriciis.

MI. Abeamus intro, ut Collybiscam vilicam

hanc perdoceamus ut ferat fallaciam.

AG. Quamquam Cupido in corde vorsatur, tamen

tibi auscultabo. **MI.** Faciam ut facto gaudeas.

50 itaque hic scelestus est homo leno Lycus,

cui iam infortuni intenta ballistast probe,

quam ego hau multo post mittam e ballistario.

sed Adelphasium eccam exit atque Anterastilis.

haec est prior quae meum erum dementem facit.

56 **tumultist:** = *tumulti est.* This genitive *tumulti* is to be taken closely with *quid:* "What of commotion," or in better English, "What commotion."

1.2

59 **negoti:** The regular long form of the genitive of *negotium* is *negotii*; this is the contracted (short) form, with only one *i.* This genitive is dependent on *vim.*

qui: The antecedent for this relative clause is unexpressed: "(He) who…"

vim: *vis, vis,* f. is usually "force" or "violence," but it can also mean "weight" or "load."

60 **comparato:** a singular future imperative of *comparo, -are,* which can be either second-person or (as here) third-person: "let him purchase."

61 **plus:** takes a partitive genitive (*negoti*) in Latin: "more (*of*) trouble."

62 *navem* and *mulierem* are the unexpressed objects of *exornare.*

64 **diei:** Take this genitive with *ad hoc:* "to this point of the day." This phrase seems to have been shortened from *ad hoc tempus diei, quod nunc est.*

65 **ex industria:** "diligently," "deliberately."

concessamus: = *concessavimus*

71 **neniam:** *nenia, -ae,* f., might mean "funeral dirge," and so *facere neniam* would be "to make (i.e., sing) a dirge for something"; here the sisters don't know how to put an end to all their primping.

72 **miror:** *miror, mirari* means "I'm amazed" and not "I wonder"; it introduces an indirect statement.

istaec: = *ista* (neuter accusative plural).

74 **cum:** "although." Where classical Latin would have a subjunctive within this *cum*-clause, Plautus uses an indicative (*habemus*).

nos habemus: *habeo me* can mean "I hold/keep myself in a certain manner." Here "I keep myself looking fine (*munditer*)."

55   sed evocabo. heus, i foras, Agorastocles!

      AG. Quid istuc tumultist, Milphio? **MI.** Em amores tuos,

      si vis spectare. **AG.** O multa tibi di dent bona,

      cum hoc mi obtulisti tam lepidum spectaculum!

1.2 [original lines 209–409, with cuts]

Adelphasium and Anterastilis are preparing themselves for the Aphrodisia, a festival in which they will become fully initiated prostitutes. The two women disagree on the topic of female beauty: Adelphasium deplores the need for constant primping and make-up while Anterastilis sees it as an essential enhancement. From his hiding place on the other side of the stage, Agorastocles hangs on Adelphasium's every word, though Milphio is much less impressed. When Agorastocles finally presents himself to his love, she scolds him for promising to free her but never doing so. Agorastocles calls on Milphio to plead with Adelphasium in his place. Milphio turns his pleadings for his master into a pass at Adelphasium, for which she wounds him appropriately. Milphio then mixes mock pleading for Agorastocles with his own contemptuous comments about Adelphasium. Only as the sisters are leaving does Agorastocles make his own direct appeal, a ridiculous line at the end of the scene.

      ADELPHASIUM. Negoti sibi qui volet vim parare,

60   navem et mulierem, haec duo comparato.

      nam nullae magis res duae plus negoti

      habent, forte si occeperis exornare.

      atque haec, ut loquor, nunc domo docta dico.

      nam nos usque ab aurora ad hoc quod diei est,

65   ex industria ambae numquam concessamus

      lavari aut fricari aut tergeri aut ornari,

      poliri, expoliri, pingi, fingi;

      nos noctes diesque omni in aetate semper

      ornamur, lavamur, tergemur, polimur.

70   neque umquam lavando et fricando

      scimus facere neniam.

      ANTERASTILIS. Miror equidem, soror, te istaec sic fabulari

      quae tam callida et docta sis et faceta.

      nam cum sedulo munditer nos habemus,

76 **cogitato:** another future imperative. Adelphasium is fond of them.

77 **modus:** *modus, -i,* m., can mean not just "manner" or "method" but also "end," "limit."
habitu: a supine ("in all things moderation is the finest thing to use"). The supine is a verbal noun (it is declined – only in the accusative and ablative – like a fourth declension noun) formed from the same stem as the perfect passive participle. It occurs in the ablative or accusative (see *captatum* at line 442) and is used with an adjective as here (*mirabile dictu* "amazing to say," *facile factu* "easy to do") or in the accusative with a verb of motion to express purpose (*persuasum amicis venerunt* "they came to persuade their friends"). "To use" is a slightly unusual meaning for *habeo, habere*.

78 This is the first of Adelphasium's moralizing and tangled tongue-twisters; the next is at line 114. Literally, "All excessive things produce an excess of trouble from themselves for people." *Nimium,* like *plus* in line 61, takes a partitive genitive.

79 **amabo:** this, along with *sis* (*si vis*), are popular ways of saying "please" in Plautus.

80 **salsa muriatica:** "salted pickled fish." Without refrigerators, the ancients had to rely much more heavily than we do on salt and smoke to preserve food. The salt, however, had to be washed out thoroughly before the food could be eaten or used. Anterastilis' point is that women, like preserved fish, take a lot of trouble before they can be enjoyed. The *salsa muriatica* are the subject of the verbs in lines 81–82 and the unexpressed object of *tangere.*

86 Milphio is always intent on food, and sarcastically praises Anterastilis' knowledge of how to soak preserved fish.

87 **ut:** = "how," introducing an indirect question.

88 **sat est:** = *satis est.*

89 **nobis:** translate as "about us."
nosmet: *-met* simply intensifies the pronoun.

90 **ergo amo te:** "Oh, thank you."

92 **ad...pacem:** *ad* expresses purpose here.
deum: = *deorum.* About a dozen second-declension words have this alternative ending for the genitive plural; *deum* and *liberum* "of children" are the most common.

93 **diem:** Latin can use the accusative to express an exclamation.

94 **dignum:** takes an ablative noun: "a day worthy of Venus (*Venere*)."
cui: the antecedent is *Venere.*

95 **num:** When *num* introduces a direct question, the expected answer is usually "no," but in Plautus' Latin this is not always true. Milphio *does* think it's time for a gift of wine.
me decet hic donari: "it is fitting that I now be rewarded."

96 **dic dare:** Understand *mihi te* after *dic* and translate *dare* as if it were a future infinitive.

98 **malum:** an idiomatic expletive used for emphasis: we might say "the devil."
sine: not the preposition "without" but a form of *sino, -ere;* it introduces a jussive noun clause whose introductory *ut* has been omitted.

99 **gnatum foret:** = *natum esset,* from *nascor, nasci* "to be born."

100 **illo:** "to that place."

101 **mantat:** "to await."

103 Adelphasium's derogatory catalog of the types of women at Venus' temple: *Proseda, -ae,* f. "one who sits in front (of a brothel)," just as "prostitute" comes from "one who stands in front." *Alica,- ae,* f., was a sort of porridge, or the wheat used in making it. *Alicarius, -a, -um* means "having to do with porridge." Apparently these women plied their trade in front of shops that sold such stuff. *Scortum, -i,* n., is another term for "prostitute." An obol is a small Greek coin, so someone who is *di-obol-arius,* "two-bit," is cheap indeed. Note the diminutives *-ol* and *-ul* (which have a derogatory force) in *servolorum* and *sordidulorum.*

75 vix aegreque amatorculos invenimus.

ADE. Ita est. verum hoc unum tamen cogitato:

modus omnibus rebus, soror, optimus est habitu;

nimia omnia nimium exhibent negoti hominibus ex se.

ANTE. Soror, cogita, amabo, item nos perhiberi

80 quam si salsa muriatica esse autumantur:

nisi multa aqua usque et diu macerantur,

olent, salsa sunt, tangere ut non velis.

eius seminis mulieres sunt:

insulsae admodum atque invenustae

85 sine munditia et sumptu.

MI. Coqua est haec quidem, Agorastocles, ut ego opinor:

scit muriatica ut maceret. AG. Quid molestus es?

ADE. Soror, parce, amabo: sat est istuc alios

dicere nobis, ne nosmet in nostra etiam vitia loquamur.

90 ANTE. Quiesco. ADE. Ergo amo te. sed hoc nunc

responde mihi: sunt hic omnia,

quae ad deum pacem oportet adesse? ANTE. Omnia accuravi.

AG. Diem pulchrum et celebrem et venustatis plenum,

dignum Venere pol, cui sunt Aphrodisia hodie.

95 MI. Iam num me decet hic donari

cado vini veteris? dic dare. nil respondes?

lingua huic excidit, ut ego opinor.

quid hic, malum, astans opstipuisti? AG. Sine amem, ne opturba ac tace.

MI. Taceo. AG. Si tacuisses, iam istuc 'taceo' non gnatum foret.

100 ANTE. Eamus, mea soror. ADE. Eho amabo, quid illo nunc properas?

ANTE. Rogas? quia erus nos apud aedem Veneris mantat. ADE. Maneat pol.

mane. turba est nunc apud aram. an te ibi vis inter istas versarier

prosedas, pistorum amicas, reginas alicarias,

servolorum sordidulorum scorta diobolaria?

105 **tun:** = *tune.*

I in malam crucem: Plautus' most frequently used curse (lines 256–257, 468) literally means "Go to bad torture," "Go to (or go hang on) a bad cross," or just "Go hang yourself!"

106 **propudium:** *propudium, -ii*, n., "wretch." Now Milphio hurls insults back at Adelphasium, accusing her of talking above her real position.

quasi: "as if."

eampse: = *eam* + *-pse*, an intensifying suffix.

ductitent: *ductito, -are* "to be in the habit of taking home (a woman) as wife or mistress."

108–109 Agorastocles will now worship Adelphasium (= *hanc*) as if she had Venus' powers.

110 **etiamne ut ames:** After Agorastocles' purpose clause in line 109, Milphio responds with another in an incredulous tone.

quidemst: = *quidem est.*

111 **quibus:** ablative of separation.

112 **ornatum:** *ornatus, -us*, m., "preparation," "costume," "get-up," "clothes."

113 **ut:** "how." Anterastilis is unhappy because of how *little* they're decked out.

114 The exact meaning of this line is open to debate, but the general idea is clear enough. Adelphasium is making another pithy but poorly worded moral ("enough is enough; nothing in excess"), which plays on the meanings of *satis*, "enough," and *satius*, "more than enough" or "preferable." Agorastocles, of course, thinks it's a philosophical gem.

116 **se:** refers to the subject of the main verb, *potest.*

117 **id:** is the "inner object" of *mentire* (= *mentiris*): "you're not lying (about) that."

119 **perdis:** "you're wasting (my time)."

120 **viderier:** an archaic form of *videri*, the passive infinitive. A more easily understood word order for this line would be *soror, credo te nunc viderier tibi satis lepide ornatam.*

122 **cordolium:** *cordolium, -ii*, n., "a feeling of grief (*dolor*) in the heart (*cor*)."

123 **innatast:** = *innata est.*

124 **fortuna…natura:** Both of these words are ablative.

125 **purpuram:** *purpura, -ae*, f., a shellfish that yielded a valuable purple dye. The word came to stand for the dye itself and finally it meant any cloth dyed purple. To wear such cloth was to flaunt one's wealth.

126 **conlinunt:** *conlino, -ere*, "to stain," "soil."

127 **factis:** *factum, -i*, n.: "through their deeds."

129 **ut:** "how."

mulsa: *mulsus, -a, -um* means "honey-flavored" or "honey-sweet." Agorastocles gushes, "What honey-sweet things she says!" and Milphio uses this as a opportunity to turn the conversation to one of his favorite subjects, food.

laterculos: *laterculus, -i*, m., a sort of cake shaped like a brick (*later, lateris*, n.), made of *sesuma*, sesame, and *papaver*, poppy-seeds; *triticum*, flour ground from wheat; and *frictas nuces*, roasted nuts.

131 **at ego amo hanc…:** This line was moved from a section earlier in Plautus' original text which we cut, but we placed it here to sum up the different love interests of Agorastocles and Milphio.

esse: an alternative form of the present active infinitive of *edo, edere.* Supply *amo* as the main verb.

132 **lubet:** = *libet* in classical Latin, and is used frequently in this play.

hac (via): [come] "*this (way).*"

105 MI. I in malam crucem! tun audes etiam servos spernere,

propudium? quasi bella sit, quasi eampse reges ductitent,

monstrum mulieris, tantilla tanta verba funditat!

AG. Iam Venus non est Venus:

hanc equidem Venerem venerabor me ut amet posthac propitia.

110 MI. Etiamne ut ames eam quam numquam tetigeris? AG. Nihil id quidemst:

deos quoque edepol et amo et metuo, quibus tamen abstineo manus.

ANTE. Eu ecastor! cum ornatum aspicio nostrum ambarum, paenitet

exornatae ut simus. ADE. Immo vero sane commode;

eo illud satiust 'satis' quod satis est habitu; hoc plus quam sat est.

115 AG. Ita me di ament!

nam illa mulier lapidem silicem subigere ut se amet potest.

MI. Pol id quidem hau mentire, nam tu es lapide silice stultior,

qui hanc ames. AG. I in malam rem. MI. Ibi sum equidem.

AG. Perdis. MI. Taceo. AG. At perpetuo volo.

120 ANTE. Satis nunc lepide ornatam credo, soror, te tibi viderier;

sed ubi exempla conferentur meretricum aliarum, ibi tibi

erit cordolium.

ADE. Invidia in me numquam innatast neque malitia, mea soror.

aurum, id fortuna invenitur, natura ingenium bonum.

125 meretricem pudorem gerere magis decet quam purpuram:

pulchrum ornatum turpes mores peius caeno conlinunt,

lepidi mores turpem ornatum facile factis comprobant.

AG. Milphio! MI. Edepol Milphionem miserum! quid nunc vis tibi?

AG. Opsecro hercle, ut mulsa loquitur! MI. Nil nisi laterculos,

130 sesumam papaveremque, triticum et frictas nuces.

AG. At ego amo hanc. MI. At ego esse et bibere.

ANTE. Eamus, mea germana. ADE. Age sis, ut lubet. ANTE. Sequere hac. ADE.

Sequor.

AG. Eunt hae. quid si adeamus? MI. Adeas. AG. Primum prima salva sis,

et secunda tu secundo salve in pretio; tertia

135 **oleum et operam perdidi:** "I've wasted my olive oil and my effort," where we might say "I've wasted my time and money." The *ancilla* in this, her only line, states that she has tried to keep herself pretty as well, but Agorastocles could care less. He dismisses her as worthless, which is a harsh, but common ancient opinion of slaves.

136 **quid eo:** "Why (are you going) to that place?"

138 **tam saeviter:** Agorastocles jokingly pretends that Adelphasium is in a huff (which she actually is).

    mitte: Understand *me* as the object of *mitte*. *Mittere* can mean "to let go."

    illi: "there."

141 **mecum caput et corpus copulas:** Agorastocles finally asks directly for what he wants. English would use a future tense instead of the present tense here.

142 This is our version (not Plautus') of the proverbial "when pigs fly." The original line was a more obscure metaphor for the same idea, "I'll never go with you." *Alacer, -cris, -cre* means "swift," "speedy." *Alacres* could agree with either *porci* or *alas*.

143 **nescioquot:** "I-do-not-know-how-many," "uncountable." This is an indeclinable adjective; here it modifies *nummi*.

    lymphatici: *lymphaticus, -a, -um* generally means "crazy," "maddened." Agorastocles' coins are "wildly" trying to be spent. We talk in English (though in different circumstances) of "mad money" or "money burning a hole in one's pocket."

144 **deferto:** another future imperative from their champion, Adelphasium.

    faxo: an old alternate for *fecero*, and it introduces a noun clause (with no introductory *ut*): "I will immediately (*actutum*) have brought it about that your madness stops," or in better English, "I'll put an end to your mad money."

145 **bellula:** a diminutive of *bella*: "What a cute gal!"

    dierecte: a word of uncertain meaning. It is used when one person dismisses another and is probably contemptuous, as also at line 20.

146 **quam magis…tam magis:** "the more…the more." *nimbata* comes from *nimbus, -i,* m., "cloud;" Milphio calls her "cloudy" or "air-headed" or "vapid."

    nugae merae: *nuga, -ae,* f., is something worthless, a trifle, a piece of trash.

147 **age:** "come on." This is put, like the English phrase "come on," before another imperative.

    amiculum: "skirt" or "cloak." This has nothing to do with *amica*, "friend," but comes from *amicio, -ire, amicui, amictum,* "to clothe."

148 **pura sum:** Adelphasium proclaims she's ritually clean (*pura*), which may also be interpreted as "I'm a good girl," or more directly, "I'm a virgin." In the strictest terms she is on her way to a ceremony for prostitutes so she is supposed to be "clean" when she sacrifices, but here in her case the word carries a double meaning since she is about to become profoundly "unclean" in her profession as a prostitute.

    comperce: can take an infinitive.

    amabo: "please," as in line 79 and throughout Plautus.

    attrectare: *attrecto, -are* "to touch," "to handle," usually in a bad sense, "to harass."

149 **agam:** like *curem* in line 150, is a deliberative subjunctive: "What should I do now?"

    facere compendi potes: *compendi facere* + accusative is an idiom for "to save oneself (the trouble of)." In a future less vivid condition, verbs such as *possum* often remain in the indicative, whereas we would say "you *could* save yourself the trouble."

135 salve extra pretium. **ANCILLA.** Tum pol ego et oleum et operam perdidi.

    AG. Quo te agis? **ADE.** Egone? in aedem Veneris. **AG.** Quid eo? **ADE.** Vt

    Venerem propitiem. **AG.** Quid tu ais? **ADE.** Quid mihi molestus es, opsecro?

    AG. Aha, tam saeviter! **ADE.** Mitte, amabo. **AG.** Quid festinas? turba nunc illi

    est. **ADE.** Scio. sunt illi aliae quas spectare ego et me spectari volo.

140 Quia apud aedem Veneris hodie est mercatus meretricius.

    AG. Vah! quid ais tu? quando illi apud me mecum caput et corpus copulas?

    ADE. Quo die porci alas alacres sibi absumpserint.

    AG. Sunt mihi intus nescioquot nummi aurei lymphatici.

    ADE. Deferto ad me, faxo actutum constiterit lymphaticum.

145 **MI.** Bellula hercle! **AG.** Abi dierecte in maximam malam crucem!

    MI. Quam magis aspecto, tam magis est nimbata et nugae merae.

    ADE. Segrega sermonem. taedet. **AG.** Age, sustolle hoc amiculum.

    ADE. Pura sum, comperce amabo me attrectare, Agorastocles.

    AG. Quid agam nunc? **ADE.** Si sapias, curam hanc facere compendi potes.

150 **ecce odium meum:** *odium* usually refers to a feeling of hatred, but it can also refer to the object (in this case, Agorastocles) that one hates.

151 **periisti:** although this verb (from *pereo, perire, peri(v)i, peritum*) is perfect when we expect a future, our English idiom is the same: "You're done for if you don't…"

152 **exora, blandire, expalpa:** Agorastocles suggests three ways for Milphio to entice Adelphasium: through prayers (*exorare*), verbal enticements (*blandiri*), and physical caresses (*expalpare*). Milphio goes too far with the last suggestion.

153 **sed vide sis ne:** *sis* (= *si vis*, "if you're willing") is another way of saying "please." *Vide ne* "watch out that you don't," "take care not to," "make sure that you don't."

   pectas: *pecto, -ere,* "to comb" (one's hair, wool, etc.), here it means "to thrash." Note how the alliteration of p's enforces the sound of the beating that Milphio will receive.

154 **in me:** *me* here is accusative, and when *in* + accusative refers to people, it often means "towards" or "against" rather than "into."

   morare: = *moraris.*

155 **multa ex multis:** *ex* can mean "after." This Latin phrase is the equivalent of our "one thing after another."

   in cassum: "to no avail," "in vain," "worthless."

157 **exspecto:** The present tense can also show an action that began in the past and is still continuing: "While I've waited for you (and I'm still waiting)…"

   copiam: *copia* can be any sort of "resource." Adelphasium means that she's found no other lover to provide her with the money to purchase her freedom.

158 **istuc:** = *istud,* "that promise of yours" (with a sneer).

   nihilo minus: literally, "none the less." In both languages, it can be written as one word (*nihilominus*, "nonetheless").

159 **apscede:** addressed to Agorastocles, and the monosyllables in *tu a me* give it extra force.

162 **meum mel, meum cor, meus molliculus caseus:** "Honey" and "(sweet)heart" were ancient terms of endearment just as they are today, but in Milphio's mind these sweet thoughts turn to his own special love of food, and he ends his speech by calling Adelphasium "my little soft cream cheese."

163 **me…praesente:** an ablative absolute: "while I am present."

   patiar: another deliberative subjunctive: "shall I allow?"

164 **suscensere:** "get angry at" (+ dative case).

165 **faciet ut sis:** "he'll bring it about that you be…" or "he'll make you a …"

166 **quin:** introduces a question that acts as a gentle command: "why don't you…" With *adire sinis*, supply *eum* as the subject of the infinitive.

   quin tibi: a more easily understood word order for this sentence would be *quin bene vis item (eis) qui bene volunt tibi?*

167 **sine:** not a preposition but the verb *sino, sinere.*

   auriculis: Milphio tries to grab her by the ears and move in for a kiss.

168 **hinc:** "from here." Remember that *sis* (= *si vis*) is another way of saying "please." Even at her most annoyed, Adelphasium is still rather courteous.

   sycophanta: *sycophanta, -ae,* m., "swindler," "cheater," "quack." Like *poeta* and *agricola,* this is another first declension word that refers to a man.

   par ero: the adjective *par, paris,* "equal," is often (as here) followed by a dative.

   scin: = *scisne.*

   at scin quo modo?: Milphio asks whether she realizes how alike he is to his master.

169 **ploratillum:** *ploratillus, -a, -um,* "inclined to weeping," "weepiful," "sob-lime," occurs nowhere else in Latin literature. Here it refers to Agorastocles. Milphio fears that his master will cry if he (Milphio) doesn't succeed.

150 **AG.** Quid? ego non te curem? quid ais, Milphio? **MI.** Ecce odium meum!

AG. Iam hercle tu periisti, nisi illam mihi tranquillam facis.

MI. Quid faciam? **AG.** Exora, blandire, expalpa. **MI.** Faciam sedulo.

sed vide sis, ne tu oratorem hunc pugnis pectas postea.

AG. Non faciam. **ADE.** Non aequus in me es, sed morare et male facis.

155 bene promittis multa ex multis: omnia in cassum cadunt.

liberare iuravisti me hau semel, sed centiens:

dum te exspecto, neque ego usquam aliam mihi paravi copiam

neque istuc usquam apparet; ita nunc servio nihilo minus.

i, soror. apscede tu a me. **AG.** Perii! ecquid ais, Milphio?

160 **MI.** Mea voluptas, mea delicia, mea vita,

meum labellum, meum savium,

meum mel, meum cor, meus molliculus caseus …

AG. Mene ego illaec patiar praesente dici?

MI. Noli, amabo, suscensere ero meo, causa mea.

165 faciet ut sis civis Attica atque libera.

quin adire sinis? quin tibi qui bene volunt, bene vis item?

sine te exorem, sine prehendam auriculis, sine dem savium.

ADE. Apscede hinc sis sycophanta par ero. **MI.** At scin quo modo?

iam hercle ego faciam ploratillum, nisi te facio propitiam,

170 **verberetillum:** *verberetillus, -a, -um* "inclined to being beaten," "wound-erful" is also a unique word.

172 **trioboli:** *triobolum, -i,* n., "three-obol coin." Three obols (an obol was a Greek coin) was quite a small amount of money and therefore represents "a pittance," "a trifle." Here it is a genitive of price or value. Agorastocles means that he won't be worth even this much if he doesn't thrash Milphio.
mastigiae: *mastigia, –ae,* f., "someone who deserves a whipping," a "rascal."

173 **em:** a shorter form of *ecce,* "look here," "behold," "here," "voilà." Agorastocles begins to beat Milphio and repeat the sweet nothings that Milphio used on Adelphasium.

175 **diceres:** a potential subjunctive that refers to the past: "You might/could have spoken like this."
huius: Agorastocles proceeds to show Milphio how Milphio should have spoken to Adelphasium by calling her "*his* (i.e., Agorastocles') delight" rather than "my (i.e., Milphio's) delight." Agorastocles is playing the part of Milphio speaking on behalf of Agorastocles, which is a ludicrous situation, but a great lesson in the difference between personal and demonstrative pronouns.

179 **atque odium meum:** Milphio approaches Adelphasium again, using the words that Agorastocles wanted, but adding his own feelings in sarcastic asides.

181 **lippitudo:** *lippitudo, lippitudinis,* m., "an inflammation or watering of the eyes."

182 **ostreatum:** *ostrea, -ae,* f., "oyster"; so *ostreatum* (a word that appears nowhere else in Latin) means "oystered," that is, striped (with welts from beatings) like an oyster. Milphio mentioned his beatings at lines 7–8 also.
gestito: = *gero.*

183 **men:** = *mene.*
prohibere: introduces two negative noun clauses separated by *magis quam.*

184 The subject of both *verberet* and *sit* is Agorastocles.
advorsum: = *adversum.* Although this word usually governs the noun or pronoun that follows, here it governs the preceding pronoun *me.*

185 Anterastilis breaks in and tells her sister to say *something* so they can leave.

188 **re divina:** "holy thing or matter, ritual" is the sisters' sacrifice at the Aphrodisia.
i: is a singular imperative. Both prostitutes are off to the festival, but Agorastocles is only concerned with one of them.
strenue: "quickly."

189 **audin:** = *audisne.* Remember that *audio* can mean either "to hear" or "to listen." Agorastocles is calling to Adelphasium as she leaves the stage.
dicito: a future imperative of *dico, -ere.*
dicito multum meis verbis salutem: *salutem dicere* is to "say hello." The lovesick Agorastocles asks Adelphasium to give a "big hello" to Venus for him.

191 **respice:** Adelphasium does not respond, but Agorastocles begs her to look back at him as she goes offstage. She does look back and Agorastocles is overjoyed.

192 **idem:** the neuter accusative singular of *idem, eadem, idem,* "the same." The point of the joke is that the verb *respicio,* literally "to look back (at)," can also mean "to show concern (for)." Agorastocles is sure that Venus will do for Adelphasium what Adelphasium did for him.
facturam: supply *esse* to complete this future infinitive.

170 atque hic ne me verberetillum faciat, nisi te propitio,

male formido.

AG. Non ego homo trioboli sum, nisi ego illi mastigiae

exturbo oculos atque dentes. em voluptatem tibi!

em mel! em cor! em labellum! em savium!

175 sic enim diceres, sceleste: huius voluptas,

huius mel, huius cor, huius labellum, huius lingua, huius savium,

huius delicia, huius dulciculus caseus, mastigia,

omnia illa, quae dicebas tua esse, ea memorares mea.

MI. Opsecro hercle te, voluptas huius atque odium meum,

180 huius amica mammeata, mea inimica et malevola,

oculus huius, lippitudo mea, mel huius, fel meum,

itaque iam quasi ostreatum tergum ulceribus gestito

propter amorem vestrum. **ADE.** Amabo, men prohibere postulas

ne te verberet magis quam ne mendax me advorsum sit?

185 **ANTE.** Aliquid huic responde, amabo, commode, ne incommodus nobis sit.

ADE. Verum. etiam tibi hanc amittam noxiam unam, Agorastocles.

non sum irata. **AG.** Non es? **ADE.** Non sum. **AG.** Da ergo, ut credam, savium.

ADE. Mox dabo, cum ab re divina rediero. **AG.** I ergo strenue. **ADE.** Sequere

me, soror.

AG. Atque audin? **ADE.** Etiam. **AG.** Veneri dicito multam meis verbis salutem.

190 **ADE.** Dicam. **AG.** Atque hoc audi.

ADE. Quid est? **AG.** Paucis verbis rem divinam facito. atque audin? respice.

respexit! idem edepol Venerem credo facturam tibi.

1.3

194 **Philippos:** see the note at line 25.

196 **per:** In the context of an oath, this preposition means "by."
dexteram: stands for *dexteram manum*, "right hand."

197 **sororem:** Agorastocles refers to his left hand as a "sister" to the right hand.

199 **Milphidisce:** Agorastocles tries to gain Milphio's favor by using a diminutive form of his name as a term of endearment: "My sweet little Milphio!"

200 **quidemst:** = *quidem est*.

201 **testis:** = *testes* (accusative plural).

203 **officium:** refers to Agorastocles' *fugio*. As a slave it is Milphio's "job" to flee.
fugio: has a double meaning here since for Agorastocles it means "I'm going," but for Milphio, as he indicates by his answer, "Hey, that's my line (my job)," it means "to flee," "to escape from one's master." Agorastocles suddenly plays the part of the slave because Milphio has taken over the role of the master by giving orders in the previous lines.

204 **ecfexis:** = *effexis* = *effeceris*, a future perfect indicative of *efficio, efficere*.

204–211 The love-struck Agorastocles is in such a daze that he is unable to finish a thought or leave the stage. Milphio tries to get him going so that they can set their trap for the pimp.

205 **emittam manu:** *emittere manu* means "to set free." Agorastocles claims that he will set Milphio free if he destroys the pimp.

207 **aquaest:** = *aquae est*.
abiturun: = *abiturusne*.

208 **pergin:** = *pergisne*.

213 **isti...orationi:** "for that speech."
Oedipo: Oedipus was a legendary king of Thebes who solved the riddle of the Sphinx, a half-woman, half-beast that killed travelers who could not answer the riddle.

214 **opust:** = *opus est*. This idiom means "there is need of" and the thing that you need (in this case, Oedipus) goes into the ablative case.

215 **illic:** = *ille*.

216 **testis:** see line 201.

1.3 [original lines 410–448, with cuts]

Agorastocles and Milphio renew their plans to trick the pimp.

MI. Quid nunc vis tibi?

AG. Trecentos Philippos Collybiscae vilicae

195 dedi dudum, prius quam me evocavisti foras.

nunc opsecro te, Milphio, hanc per dexteram

perque hanc sororem laevam perque oculos tuos

perque tuam libertatem … MI. Em nunc nihil opsecras.

AG. Mi Milphidisce, mea commoditas, mea salus,

200 fac ut ego hunc lenonem perdam. MI. Perfacile id quidemst.

i, adduce testis tecum; ego intus interim

tuam exornabo vilicam. propera atque abi.

AG. Fugio. MI. Meum est istuc magis officium quam tuum.

AG. Egone, egone, si istuc lepide ecfexis … MI. I modo.

205 AG. Emittam manu …

MI. Abi modo.

AG. Neque quantum aquaest in mari … MI. Abiturun es?

AG. Neque nubes omnes quantumst … MI. Pergin pergere?

AG. Neque stellae in caelo … MI. Pergin auris tundere?

210 AG. Neque hoc neque illud neque … enim vero serio …

quod hic inter nos liceat … ita me Iuppiter …

MI. Si nequeo facere ut abeas, egomet abiero;

nam isti quidem hercle orationi Oedipo

opust coniectore, qui Sphingi interpres fuit!

215 AG. Illic hinc iratus abiit.

ibo atque arcessam testis, quando Amor iubet

me oboedientem esse servo liberum.

2.1

218 **infelicent:** *infelico, -are,* "to make *infelix*" or "to curse."

    qui: a relative adjective ("who") that agrees with *leno* and whose antecedent is *illum.*

219 **immolarit:** = *immolaverit;* future perfect, since Lycus imagines sacrifices completed in the future.

220 **meis:** Lycus says "my gods" because each person, according to his or her profession, could pray to a specific set of gods. For example, merchants would naturally pray to Mercury, and Lycus, being a pimp and involved in matters of love, has sacrificed to Venus.

222 **uti esset:** parenthetical, as if Lycus had said *facere ut Venus propitia esset mihi.*

223 **nequeo:** is used here in an historical present. We logically translate this verb as a past tense ("I was unable"), but in Latin it appears in the present tense.

    illim: = *illinc,* "from that place."

    ilico: "at that place," or, of time, "on the spot" as in line 247.

224 **exta:** *exta, -orum,* n. pl., "upper internal organs," especially the heart, lungs, and liver. They were used in telling the future and often given to the *haruspex* (a religious official trained to detect perfection or blemishes in the organs in order to determine whether a good or bad future would exist for the patron) as a payment for his services. But Lycus got a bad reading so he wouldn't let the *haruspex* keep the choice organs. Sacrificers might save organs and meat for their own consumption at home or leave some for the gods and their priests.

    prosicarier: the archaic form of the present passive infinitive (= *prosecari*).

225 **adii manum:** *adeo manum* is an idiomatic way of saying "to trick" or "to deceive." The object of the trick or deception goes in the dative case.

226 **noluit:** Venus is the subject.

    habere: here means "consider," as in the English phrase, "We <u>hold</u> these truths to be self-evident." The phrase *habere satis* means "to consider sufficient" or "to be content with."

228 **condigne:** "worthily, fittingly." Lycus is sarcastic since this applies to the *haruspex* who refused to read Lycus' future the way he wanted it read.

    trioboli: as at line 172, *triobolum, -i,* n., a "three-obol coin." Three obols was a small amount of money and, as a genitive of price or value, describes the *haruspex* whom Lycus considers "worthless."

229 **portendi:** *portendo, -ere,* "to portend, reveal by means of omens." Here it is a passive infinitive in indirect speech.

231 **quid ei divini aut humani:** The interrogative pronoun *quid* is followed by two partitive genitives. The direct object of *credere* is *quid* and the indirect object is *ei.*

    aequumst: = *aequum est,* often used to introduce indirect statements. The whole line literally means "What of the divine (what divine thing) or of the human (what human thing) is it reasonable to entrust to him?"

232 **mina:** a Greek measure of weight here designating a large sum of Greek silver coinage. It is a considerable sum of money for the pimp to receive. This explains why Lycus refers to the *haruspex* as worth a tiny sum of money (*trioboli*) since the soothsayer failed to predict this huge windfall.

    dono: a dative of purpose, "for a gift." Lycus is exaggerating since the soldier clearly expects to be fed and entertained in return for his "gift."

233 **illic:** a stronger form of *ille.*

    restitit: *resto, -are, restiti,* "to remain, stay put."

235 **ut:** "as."

236 **pugna Panamanica:** Plautus' original imaginary campaign here was a *pugna Pentetronica.* We changed this to suggest the forgettable "Operation Just Cause," the search for Manuel Noriega in Panama.

2.1 [original lines 449–503]

Lycus the pimp has spent the morning in town at the Aphrodisia, where he had been sacrificing to Venus, the goddess of his profession. He is, however, sick of the haruspices, those readers of signs from the innards of animals, who always predict doom for him. Lycus believes that he is faring quite well since he has already received some money today from a soldier, Antamoenides, who loves to talk of his exploits. Lycus is far from impressed with the soldier's tale of killing flying men, and, instead, openly scoffs at the miles. Despite a brief flash of anger at this disbelieving pimp, the blowhard soldier is ready for some action and so follows Lycus into his "den of iniquity."

> LYCUS. Di illum infelicent omnes, qui post hunc diem
>
> leno ullam Veneri umquam immolarit hostiam.
>
> 220 nam ego hodie infelix dis meis iratissumis
>
> sex immolavi agnos nec potui tamen
>
> propitiam Venerem facere uti esset mihi.
>
> quoniam litare nequeo, abii illim ilico
>
> iratus, votui exta prosicarier;
>
> 225 eo pacto avarae Veneri pulchre adii manum.
>
> quando id quod sat erat satis habere noluit,
>
> ego pausam feci. sic ago, sic me decet.
>
> condigne haruspex, non homo trioboli,
>
> omnibus in extis aibat portendi mihi
>
> 230 malum damnumque et deos esse iratos mihi.
>
> quid ei divini aut humani aequumst credere?
>
> mina mihi argenti dono postilla datast.
>
> sed quaeso, ubinam illic restitit miles modo
>
> qui hanc mihi donavit, quem ego vocavi ad prandium?
>
> 235 sed eccum incedit. ANTAMOENIDES. Ita ut occepi dicere,
>
> lenulle, de illa pugna Panamanica,
>
> cum sexaginta milia hominum uno die
>
> volaticorum manibus occidi meis.
>
> LY. Volaticorum ... hominum? ANTA. Ita dico quidem.

240 **an:** here introducing a single direct question when the questioner is surprised, as Lycus is.

usquam sunt…: "Have there ever been flying men?" Latin uses the present tense to refer to action that continues into the present, whereas English uses the present perfect.

241 **fuerunt:** "There *were*"; perfect tense because the flying men no longer exist.

242–248 Antamoenides claims that he instructed his men to load their slings (*funda, -ae*, f.) with bird-lime (*viscum, -i*, n.), a sticky substance more usually smeared on branches to trap the birds unlucky enough to land on them. He had them put leaves (*folium, -i*, n.) of the broad-leaved plant coltsfoot (*farferum, -i*, n.) in the slings to keep the bird-lime from sticking to the slings. The flying men were then to be hit (*fundito, -are*, "to propel by means of a sling") with globs of the lime, to make them fall. Antamoenides' plan for killing the flying men is just as fantastical as the existence of the flying men in the first place.

243 **eo:** "there" (i.e., "in the slings").

praesternebant: *praesterno, -ere*, "to strew in front." Here used of spreading the leaves in the front of the slings.

245 **grandiculos:** *grandiculus, -a, -um*. An odd combination of *grandis* (big) with the diminutive suffix *-ulus*. Hence "fair-sized," "pretty big."

246 **eo:** the ablative of *id* meaning "with that."

volantis = *volantes* (accusative plural).

funditarier: = *funditari*, archaic passive infinitive like *prosicarier* at line 224.

247 **ut quisque acciderat:** The pluperfect indicative after *ut* can be translated as if it were perfect: "Whenever one fell."

251 **mi haec non credis:** *credo* is used here with both an adverbial accusative and a dative indirect object: "You don't believe me" + "you don't believe these things."

252 **dum exta referuntur:** Antamoenides is referring to the *exta* being brought back from the sacrifice for consumption as described at line 224.

253 **nil moror:** *moror* is here intransitive; *nil* (= *nihil*) functions as an adverb: "I'm not waiting."

255 **colaphis:** *colaphus, -i*, m., "a blow struck with the fist."

dilidam: *dilido, dilidere*, "to batter into pieces."

256 **aut auscultas aut…is in malem crucem:** an illogical pairing due to Antamoenides' flustered anger: "I'll kill you if you don't listen or…go hang yourself (first)." For going *in malam crucem* see line 105.

257 **malam crucem ibo:** supply *in* from the line above. Lycus sarcastically responds that he'd rather go hang himself than listen to more of Antamoenides' war stories.

certumnest tibi: literally, "Is it certain to you?" or in better English, "Are you sure?"

259 **tuam…meretricem minusculam:** Lycus' "slightly younger/smaller" prostitute is of course Anterastilis, as contrasted with Adelphasium who is *maiusculam* (see line 15).

260 **sequere:** the imperative, not an infinitive.

hac: = *hac via*: "Follow me this way," as at line 132.

261 **in hunc diem:** "for this day."

240 LY. An, opsecro, usquam sunt homines volatici?

ANTA. Fuerunt. verum ego interfeci. LY. Quo modo

potuisti? ANTA. Dicam. viscum legioni dedi

fundasque; eo praesternebant folia farferi.

LY. Perge. optume hercle peiieras. quid postea?

245 ANTA. In fundas visci indebant grandiculos globos,

eo illos volantis iussi funditarier.

ut quisque acciderat, eum necabam ilico

per cerebrum pinna sua sibi quasi turturem.

LY. Si hercle istuc umquam factum est, tum me Iuppiter

250 faciat ut semper sacruficem nec umquam litem.

ANTA. An mi haec non credis? LY. Credo, ut mi aequumst credier.

age eamus intro. ANTA. Dum exta referuntur, volo

narrare tibi etiam unam pugnam. LY. Nil moror.

ANTA. Ausculta. LY. Non hercle auscultabo. ANTA. Quo modo?

255 colaphis quidem hercle tuum iam dilidam caput,

nisi aut auscultas aut … is in malam crucem.

LY. Malam crucem ibo potius. ANTA. Certumnest tibi?

LY. Certum. ANTA. Tum tu igitur die bono, Aphrodisiis,

addice tuam mihi meretricem minusculam.

260 LY. Nunc hinc eamus intro. sequere hac me. ANTA. Sequor.

in hunc diem iam tuus sum mercennarius.

3.1

262 **ita me di ament:** an oath; our English parallel is "So help me, God."

nihil est quicquam: Forms of *quisquam* are often used to strengthen *nihil*, somewhat redundantly: "nothing at all."

nequius: the comparative form of *nequam*.

263 **homini amanti:** with *nequius*. "Nothing is more useless, especially for a man in love."

264 **sicut:** "Just as now." Agorastocles applies the general concept to his specific case.

advocatos: Literally, "those who have been called in." In Plautus' day *advocati* were professional "assistants, helpers, or witnesses (Latin, *testes*)." As hired professional witnesses, these *advocati* will prove untrustworthy. They are members of the lowly freed class (just above slaves) and are almost as interested in food as Milphio.

spissigradissimos: from *spissus, -a, -um*, "sluggish," "slow"; *gradior, gradiri*, "to walk"; and the superlative *-issimus*: "extremely slow-stepping."

265 **corbitae:** *corbita, -ae*, f., "a slow-moving merchant ship," "barge."

266 **procos:** *procus, -i*, m., usually means "suitor," but here it means "nobleman." It is a sarcastic remark by Agorastocles since the *advocati* were only freedmen. They respond indignantly at lines 269ff.

loripedes: *loripes, loripedis*, an adjective, seems to mean "having a deformity of the foot."

267 **si ituri…estis:** the future participle of *eo, ire* used with the verb to be. "If you are (going) to come…"

in malam crucem: as at line 256, "(go) to hell."

269 **salve, salve, salve:** This is our replacement of Plautus' *Heus tu*, "Hey you." We made the change to give each of our three *advocati* a chance to introduce her- or himself with a Latin version of the Three Stooges' familiar musical greeting, "Hello, Hello, Hello."

plebeii: *plebeius, -a, -um*, "belonging to the common people."

270 **si nec recte dicis nobis:** "and if you don't speak correctly (i.e., nicely) to us…"

dives: vocative case.

271 The *advocati* break off the conditional sentence, but make their threat clear enough: "If you, snooty rich guy, don't treat us right…we routinely punish the rich."

mactare: *macto, -are* can mean "to honor," "to punish," or "to sacrifice"; here "punish," with an ablative of means.

infortunio: *infortunium, -ii*, n., "misfortune," "unhappiness."

272 **obnoxii:** *obnoxius, -a, -um*, "answerable to," "accountable to." Grammatically, it works with the dative *tibi* and an inner (adverbial) accusative *istuc* (= *istud*), which introduces a relative clause of characteristic: "Nor are we answerable to you regarding what you love or hate." They do not care whether he loves them or hates them.

oderis: *odi, -isse*, "to hate"; perfect subjunctive equivalent in sense to a present subjunctive since *odi* has no present tense forms (it's a 'defective' verb) and its perfect tense has a present meaning.

273 The *advocati* have spent their own money to free themselves, so they ought to be free. As freedmen at Rome their rights would have been somewhat restricted, and they are clearly anxious to be treated as fully free men, not as the slaves they once were.

pendimus: *pendo, -ere*, "to weigh," "to value."

nihili: genitive of price; compare *trioboli* in line 228.

274 **ne…censeas:** a negative command loosely attached as a negative purpose clause: "We don't care about you so don't think…," i.e., "and we say this so you won't think…"

3.1 [original lines 504–577]

Agorastocles returns from town with a trio of professional witnesses. He considers them lazy shufflers who move only when they're offered food. The witnesses are proud of their freed status and complain that Agorastocles treats them like slaves. Agorastocles asks them to rehearse their part (they are there to observe Lycus taking Agorastocles' slave into his house), which they mime to perfection.

       AG. Ita me di ament, tardo amico nihil est quicquam nequius,

       praesertim homini amanti, qui, quidquid agit, properat omnia.

       sicut ego hos duco advocatos, homines spissigradissimos,

265   tardiores quam corbitae sunt in tranquillo mari.

       nequiquam hos procos mi elegi loripedes, tardissumos.

       quin, si ituri hodie estis, ite, aut ite hinc in malam crucem.

       nonne cum pedicis condidicistis istoc grassari gradu?

       ADVOCATI. Salve, salve, salve. quamquam nos videmur tibi plebeii et

270   pauperes, si nec recte dicis nobis, dives, de summo loco,

       divitem audacter solemus mactare infortunio.

       nec tibi nos obnoxii istuc quid tu ames aut oderis:

       liberos nos esse oportet. nos te nihili pendimus,

       ne tuo nos amori servos tuos esse addictos censeas.

275 **magis par est:** The subject of *est* is the accusative and infinitive phrase (*liberos … ire*): "to go at a moderate pace is more fitting for free men."

modico: *modicus, -a, -um,* "moderate."

gradu: *gradus, -us,* m., "step," "pace"; ablative of manner with *modico.*

276 **servile…currere:** The *advocati* explain that they will not run around to do work for Agorastocles because that would be acting as if they were still slaves, not freedmen. This would especially be true for the stage world in which the *advocati* are playing, since slaves running about performing tasks for their masters are common in Roman comedy.

duco: here means "consider," introducing an indirect statement whose main verb is *esse.*

278 **pridie:** "the day before."

duxisse oportuit: Strictly speaking, the perfect infinitive is overkill after the perfect *oportuit,* but this particular construction is common in Plautus. It is fitting here, as the *advocati* want to make it clear that Agorastocles ought to have summoned them before now if he's in such a hurry.

279 **ne tu opinere:** a negative command. The phrase is apparently parenthetical here, having no effect on the future indicative *curret.*

280 **ad prandium…in aedem:** "to (my) house for lunch." "Lunch" is a key word for it is part of what motivates the *advocati* to work for Agorastocles. The *parasitus,* "mooch," "leech," "hanger on," was a standard character in Plautine comedy. He was a freedman motivated mostly by the promise of food from a wealthier patron. In this play the *advocati* fill that role, but they also share it to some degree with the slave Milphio who also loves food. In the comic world, therefore, many freedmen are slavish in their qualities and passions, showing that a change of status did not necessarily mean a change in habits.

me…dixissem ducere: *dixissem* introduces the accusative *me* and infinitive *ducere* of an indirect statement.

281 **vinceretis:** This imperfect subjunctive along with the pluperfect subjunctive *dixissem* creates a mixed contrary-to-fact condition: If Agorastocles had *previously* invited the *advocati* to lunch, they would *now* still be speeding along.

cervum: *cervus, -i,* m., "deer."

cursu: *cursus, -us,* m., "the action of running"; ablative of respect, as is *gradu.*

gralatorem: *gralator, -oris,* m., "stilt-walker." Agorastocles says that the *advocati* would have taken even bigger steps than someone on stilts.

282 **ducere:** Supply *me* (from line 280) as the accusative subject of this indirect statement: "Because I said I was leading you here as my advocates and witnesses…"

283 **podagrosi:** *podager, -gra, -grum,* "suffering from gout," a disease that causes painful swelling in the joints, especially in the feet.

cocleam: *coclea, -ae,* f., "snail."

tarditudine: *tarditudo, -inis,* f., "slowness."

284 **curratur:** impersonal passive; literally, "there is running," "people run." It is subjunctive in an indirect question.

285 **de alieno:** *alienum, -i,* n., "someone else's property"; *de* means "at the expense of."

ad fatim: an adverbial phrase meaning "amply," "sufficiently."

286 **cum eo cum quiqui:** a cumbersome legal phrase, "with one thing, with another," "taking all things into consideration;" *quiqui* is an old ablative form of *quisque.*

287 **contemptim:** "contemptuously."

conteras: *contero, -ere,* "to crush, wear out, treat scornfully." It is subjunctive because it is a negative command.

289 **tua causa:** ablative of cause: "because of you," "for your sake."

nostrorumst: = *nostrorum est.*

rupturus: *rumpo, -ere, rupi, ruptus,* "to rupture," "burst."

clunes: *clunis, -is,* m., "buttock." Plautus wrote *ramites,* "lungs," which we changed in order to use the modern idiom of "not busting your butt for someone," which is far more accessible than Plautus' "busting your lungs for someone."

275   liberos homines per urbem modico magis par est gradu

      ire, servile esse duco festinantem currere.

      sed si properabas magis,

      pridie nos te advocatos huc duxisse oportuit.

      ne tu opinere, hau quisquam hodie nostrum curret per vias.

280   AG. At si ad prandium me in aedem vos dixissem ducere,

      vinceretis cervum cursu vel gralatorem gradu;

      nunc vos quia mihi advocatos dixi et testis ducere,

      podagrosi estis ac vicistis cocleam tarditudine.

      ADV. An vero non iusta causa est cur curratur celeriter

285   ubi bibas, edas de alieno quantum velis usque ad fatim?

      sed tamen cum eo cum quiqui, quamquam sumus pauperculi,

      ne nos tam contemptim conteras.

      sed si properas, cursores meliust te advocatos ducere.

      tua causa nemo nostrorumst suos rupturus clunes.

290 **per iocum:** "in jest," "as a joke."

291 **itidem:** "in the same way" (*ita* + *-dem*).

habeto: The future imperative of *habere* means "consider"; here it introduces an indirect statement with *dictum* (= *dictum esse*).

292 **quod vestra opera mi[hi] opus sit:** an indirect question. The idiom *opus est*, "there is need of," uses the ablative for the thing needed (*vestra opera*) and the dative for the person who needs it: "What need there is of your work for me," i.e., "what I need you to do for me."

294 **ut:** "how," introducing an indirect question.

servo meo: Collybisca, Agorastocles' female slave, whom Milphio already made plans to disguise as a male to trick the pimp (lines 28ff). Agorastocles uses the masculine here because he is talking to the *advocati* about Collybisca as part of the scheme, not as her real female self.

295 **si...sciant:** = *si modo sciant*, "provided the spectators know." Plautus often drops the dramatic illusion by having his characters address the audience. Here the *advocati* repeat to each other the plan to trick Lycus. This often excessive repetition of the scheme is common in Plautus and may have been a way of keeping the rowdy audiences of his day attuned to the plot. The *advocati* make a joke out of this convention by saying, "Sure, we know the plot, just make sure the audience does."

296 **hic:** "here."

causa: "for the sake of," with the genitive *horum spectatorum*.

agitur: "is being acted." Our word "actor" comes from *ago, -ere, egi, actus*.

297 **curassis:** = *curaveris*, a perfect subjunctive in a negative command. *curo, -are*, "to care for," "to worry about."

297–298 **scimus rem...possemus tibi:** another meta-theatrical joke (meta-theatrical meaning a situation where the actors drop the pretense that they are characters and acknowledge their status as actors). The *advocati* answer that Agorastocles should know that they are familiar with their part in the plot (and the play) since they all rehearsed their lines at the same time.

quippe: "since."

298 **tecum una:** "at the same time as you"; literally, "together with you."

ut: "how"

299 **ita profecto est:** "that's surely right."

299–300 **agite...rem expedite:** We altered this line from Plautus' original to relate that old joke line, "So I know that you know that I know that you know..."

301 **temptas:** *temptare*, "to try to find out," followed by an indirect question with *an*, "whether."

[Mime]: In order to avoid a third retelling of the plot, we took our cue from *agite* (line 299), with its double meaning of "Come on!" and "Act out!" and subsituted a mime of the trick, which is described in the director's notes.

303 **vix quidem:** "oh, hardly." This is sarcastic, as the rest of the line shows.

digitulis primoribus: *digitulus, -i*, m., "little (i.e., small, tender) finger"; *primoris, -e*, "first, extreme, tip of": "with the tips of (our) little fingers." They can grasp this simple plot with their finger tips. Latin at times uses an adjective to describe a part of something when English would use a phrase with the genitive: *in media urbe*, "in the middle of the city."

304 **cito et cursim:** two adverbs, each meaning "quickly": *cito* from *citus* (which is in turn the perfect participle of *cieo*, "to put in motion"); *cursim* from *curro*, "to run."

305 **euge:** a Latin transliteration of a Greek expression meaning "well indeed." In Plautus' time Greek was still spoken in many cities in southern Italy that had been founded as Greek colonies.

una et: "together with."

vilica: On the gender and meaning of this word, see the note on line 28.

306 **ad fallaciam:** "for (the purpose of) deceit."

290   **AG.** Nimis iracundi estis: equidem haec vobis dixi per iocum.

     ADV. Per iocum itidem dictum habeto quae nos tibi respondimus.

     AG. Scitis rem, narravi vobis quod vestra opera mi opus sit,

     de lenone hoc qui me amantem ludificatur tam diu,

     ei paratae ut sint insidiae de auro et de servo meo.

295   **ADV.** Omnia istaec scimus iam nos, si hi spectatores sciant;

     horum hic nunc causa haec agitur spectatorum fabula.

     nos tu ne curassis: scimus rem omnem, quippe omnes simul

     didicimus tecum una, ut respondere possemus tibi.

     AG. Ita profecto est. sed agite igitur, ut sciam vos scire

300   me scire vosmet scire, rem expedite.

     ADV. Itane? temptas an sciamus? non meminisse nos ratus es?

     [**Mime**]   **AG.** Tenetis rem.

     ADV. Vix quidem hercle digitulis primoribus.

     AG. Hoc cito et cursim est agendum. properate iam quantum potest.

305   Euge! opportune egrediuntur Milphio una et vilica.

     basilice exornata incedit et fabre ad fallaciam.

3.2

308 **vide sis:** "see (to it), please, that…" (+ subjunctive).

310 **proba…probus:** Milphio slips up for a moment on his own trick of making Collybisca a male, a mistake that he quickly covers up with an emphatic *homost* (= *homo est*). For the original creation of this scheme, see the note on lines 28ff.

311 **magis…idoneos:** "better suited."

312 **cum eo cum quiqui:** "with one thing, with another"; see the note on line 286.

314 **negoti:** = *negotii*. Take this partitive genitive with *quid sit* to mean "what (of) business there is," "what the deal is," "what's up."

318 **praeceptumst:** = *praeceptum est.*

hic: Agorastocles refers to Collybisca as a man, as part of the plot to fool Lycus.

321 **agite:** Imperative forms of *agere* are often used in conjunction with other imperatives and can be translated, "Come on!" or "Lets go."

aurum…comicum: The *advocati* show the audience the fake money in Collybisca's purse.

322 **ad hanc rem agundam:** an example of the gerundive introduced by *ad* expressing purpose: "for the purpose of conducting this business." *agundam* = *agendam.*

Philippum: see note at line 25 for information on these gold coins, called *Philippi.*

323 **adsimulatote:** plural future imperative of *adsimulo, -are.*

325 **liberum:** "free" from restraints that might get in the way of a good time.

326 **potes:** from *poto, -are,* "to drink," not *possum, posse,* "to be able."

pergraecere: = *pergraeceris. pergraeco, -are* means "to behave like a Greek," probably by doing something scandalous.

327 **quis te porro:** assume *docuit* as the verb.

agite…abite: plural imperatives perhaps because Collybisca is also thinking of Milphio when she tells Agorastocles to depart.

329 **fores hae:** Collybisca points to the door (*hae*) of Lycus' house, which creaks as it opens. The creaking door is a commonplace of the Plautine stage and it allows the actor to tell the audience that he knows someone is coming onto stage and he will have to hide if he doesn't want to be detected.

3.2 [original lines 578–614, with cuts]

Milphio appears with Collybisca, who is dressed as a soldier to add to her disguise as a foreigner unknown to Lycus. Milphio is immediately put off by Agorastocles' poor choice of witnesses, but finds that they and Collybisca know their roles and are ready to set the trap for the pimp. The witnesses enjoy themselves immensely in describing all the bad things that they will help Collybisca learn for her role as a pleasure-seeker at a brothel.

MI. Iam tenes praecepta in corde? COLLYBISCA. Pulchre.

MI. Vide sis calleas. Fac modo ut condocta tibi sint dicta ad hanc fallaciam.

CO. Quin edepol condoctior sum, quam tragoedi aut comici.

310 MI. Proba … prob*us* homost. AG. Adeamus propius. adsunt testes? MI. Tot quidem.

AG. Non potuisti adducere homines magis ad hanc rem idoneos?

ADV. Di te perdant! MI. Vos quidem hercle! cum eo cum quiqui tamen

et bene et benigne facitis cum ero amanti operam datis.

sed isti iam sciunt negoti quid sit? AG. Omne in ordine.

315 MI. Tum vos animum advortite igitur. hunc vos lenonem Lycum

novistis? ADV. Facile. CO. At pol ego eum, qua sit facie, nescio.

eum mihi volo demonstretis hominem. ADV. Nos curabimus.

satis praeceptumst. AG. Hic trecentos nummos numeratos habet.

ADV. Ergo nos inspicere oportet istuc aurum, Agorastocles,

320 ut sciamus quid dicamus mox pro testimonio.

CO. Agite, inspicite. ADV. Aurum est profecto hic, spectatores, comicum:

verum ad hanc rem agundam Philippum est: ita nos adsimulabimus.

CO. Sed ita adsimulatote quasi ego sim peregrinus. ADV. Scilicet,

et quidem quasi tu nobiscum adveniens hodie oraveris

325 liberum ut commostraremus tibi locum et voluptarium

ubi ames, potes, pergraecere. CO. Eu, edepol mortales malos!

AG. Ego enim docui. MI. Quis te porro? CO. Agite intro abite, Agorastocles.

AG. Sed … ADV. I! AG. Tamen … vae mihi! CO. St, tacete.

ADV. Quid est? CO. Fores hae fecerunt magnum flagitium modo.

330 **pone:** not from *pono, -ere*; preposition with accusative, meaning "behind."

331 **illic:** = *ille.*

332 **bonus:** "fine" in the sense of "what an excellent specimen." Lycus is so evil-looking that he is a superb example of the wicked pimp.

   malist: = *mali est.* Latin uses the genitive with *similis* to mean "similar *to* someone."

3.3

333 **istuc:** "to that place where you are"; Lycus, as he comes onstage from his house, speaks (for two lines) to the soldier inside.

   revertar: *revertor, -i, reversus sum,* "to turn around and come back," "to return."

   convivas: *conviva, -ae,* m. (and f.), "table companion," "guest."

334 **qui una sint:** "who will be together," i.e., "to join us"; relative clause of purpose.

335 **quid...tantum hominum:** *hominum* is a partitive genitive: "why is such a great amount of men...?" i.e., "why are all these people...?"

   ecquidnam: *ecquis, -id* with suffix *-nam*; an emphatic form of the interrogative pronoun: "is there anything that...?" i.e., "bringing something, are they?"

   adferunt: "bring"; here it is closer to "offer," or even "have something in mind."

336 **chlamydatus:** from *chlamys,* a type of military cloak; *chlamydatus, -a, -um* means "wearing a *chlamys,*" which is simply Lycus' way of saying Collybisca is dressed like a soldier.

337 **Aetoli:** *Aetolus, -a ,-um,* "Aetolian." Aetolia is the region in western Greece in which the city of Calydon, the scene of the play, is located.

338 **inviti:** *invitus, -a, -um,* "unwilling"; best translated as an adverb, "unwillingly."

339 **sitis:** subjunctive in a wish.

   quod: "which"; both *quod* and *id* (in the next line) refer to the content of Lycus' wish.

340 **fore:** alternative form of the future infinitive of *sum,* in an indirect statement.

   situram: *sino, -ere, sivi, situs,* "to allow"; future infinitive (without *esse*) governing *fieri.*

341–342 The *advocati* compare two infinitives used as substantives, each with an adverb (*bene facere* and *male facere,* "to treat well" and "to treat badly"). Each infinitive has an indirect object expressed by an adjective in the dative case (*malo,* "a bad man," and *bono,* "a good man").

   tantundemst: = *tantumdem est,* where *tantum + dem* means "just as great." "To treat a bad man well is just as much a risk (just as dangerous) as to treat a good man badly."

343 **dictum:** Supply *est*: "That was cleverly said."

   quid: "why," or "how."

   attinet: *attineo, -ere, -ui, attentum,* "to pertain." "How does that (*istuc*) concern me?"

345 **leniter:** adverb from *lenis, -e,* "gently, moderately, slightly."

346 **quid boni:** partitive genitive, "anything of good," or "anything good." *quid* here is *aliquid* (Remember that after *si, nisi, non,* and *ne,* all the *ali-*'s drop away). Supply *quid* with the *boni* in the next line as well.

347 **de nostro:** "from ours," i.e., "at our expense."

348 **adeo:** "thus," "in this way."

330 **ADV.** Pone nos recede. **CO.** Fiat. **ADV.** Nos priores ibimus.

     ADV. Illic homo est qui egreditur leno.

     CO. Bonus est, nam similis malist.

3.3 [original 615–710, with cuts]

The witnesses tell Lycus that Collybisca (now disguised as a man) is a foreign soldier who has arrived in town in search of a good time. This is all very appealing to Lycus, and when Collybisca shows him the gold, the pimp is beside himself with excitement. The witnesses call out to Agorastocles to see Lycus leading Collybisca off into his house, thus appearing to steal Agorastocles' property.

     LY. Iam ego istuc revertar, miles: convivas volo

     reperire nobis commodos qui una sint;

335 sed quid huc tantum hominum incedunt? ecquidnam adferunt?

     et ille chlamydatus quisnam est qui sequitur procul?

     ADV. Aetoli cives te salutamus, Lyce,

     quamquam hanc salutem ferimus inviti tibi.

     LY. Fortunati omnes sitis, quod certo scio

340 nec fore nec Fortunam id situram fieri.

     ADV. Malo bene facere tantundemst periculum

     quantum bono male facere.

     LY. Facete dictum. sed quid istuc ad me attinet?

     ADV. Quia nos honoris tui causa ad te venimus,

345 quamquam bene volumus leniter lenonibus.

     LY. Si quid boni adportatis, habeo gratiam.

     ADV. Boni de nostro tibi nec ferimus nec damus

     neque pollicemur neque adeo volumus datum.

     LY. Credo hercle vobis: ita vestra est benignitas. sed

350 **hanc...hunc** The *advocati* momentarily forget that Collybisca is posing as a male soldier, just as Milphio forgot at line 310.

351 **ei:** "at him."

iratust: = *iratus est.*

capiti vestro istuc quidem: a wish, without the verb: "(May) that (fall) on your head," i.e., "the same to you."

352 **diripiundum:** *diripio, -ere*, "to tear to shreds." It is a gerundive (*diripiundum = diripiendum*) with *hunc* expressing purpose. The *advocati* want Lycus to think that Collybisca is ripe for ripping off, but the gerundive could just as well refer to Lycus, as its position next to *te* shows. "We've brought him to you for a rip-off."

353 **cum:** the preposition.

praeda: *praeda, -ae*, f., "plunder," "prey."

domum: With a verb of motion (*incedet*), this needs no preposition (*ad* or *in*).

354 **plagas:** *plaga, -ae*, f., "net." Nets were often used for hunting in antiquity.

lepide: "charmingly," "beautifully."

lupum: *lupus, -i*, m., "wolf." Collybisca's joke depends on the fact that Lycus' name means "wolf" in Greek.

356 **nisi:** "except that."

dudum: "a little while ago," "just now."

mane: not a form of *maneo, -ere*, but an adverb: "in the morning."

ut: since *processimus* is in the indicative, *ut* means "as" or "when."

357 **atque:** here means "lo and behold."

oneraria: *onerarius, -a, -um*, "cargo-bearing."

358 **peregrinum:** *peregrinus, -a, -um*, "foreigner."

360 **praeberier:** *praebeo, -ere*, "to bring forward," "to provide"; archaic form of the passive infinitive (= *praeberi*) introduced by *velle*, which is itself a main verb of the indirect statement that began in the previous line.

liberum: "free" of all possible restrictions and restraints. The soldier is looking for a place where he can indulge all his desires and enjoy himself to the fullest.

ubi nequam faciat: *nequam*, "useless," "depraved," "naughty," is an indeclinable adjective. *ubi* introduces a relative clause of purpose: "a place to fool around in."

364 **clam, furtim:** "secretly," "furtively." The *advocati* say this because they want Lycus to entertain Collybisca privately (i.e., inside his house) where he can be caught in possession of Agorastocles' slave, rather than in a more public place outside.

ne quis sciat: negative purpose clause. *quis* = *aliquis*, "anyone."

365 **neve:** *ne* + *-ve* continues the negative purpose clause.

arbiter: *arbiter, -tri*, m., "eyewitness," "witness."

latro: *latro, latronis*, m. "mercenary soldier."

Fayettevilla, Forti Braggi: We gave Plautus some North Carolina local color since we performed this originally for North Carolinians. Plautus originally made Collybisca a mercenary from Sparta, but we turned the reference into her being stationed at North Carolina's most famous military base, Ft. Bragg in Fayetteville. We apologize for misusing *fortis* just because it sounded like "Fort."

367 **multa bona dent:** *bona* are good things. The subjunctive indicates a wish.

cum: "since"; *cum* in this meaning can introduce the indicative in Plautus.

368 **praecipitis:** *praecipio, -ere*, "to take beforehand," "to anticipate," "to give advice."

369 **Philippos:** see the note at line 25.

350 quid nunc vultis? **ADV.** Hanc … *hunc* chlamydatum servum quem vides,

ei Mars iratust. **CO.** Capiti vestro istuc quidem!

ADV. Nunc hunc, Lyce, ad te diripiundum adducimus.

CO. Cum praeda hic hodie incedet venator domum:

canes compellunt in plagas lepide lupum.

355 **LY.** Quis hic est? **ADV.** Nescimus nos quidem istum qui sit;

nisi dudum mane ut ad portum processimus,

atque istum e navi exeuntem oneraria

videmus. Ait se peregrinum esse

huius ignarum oppidi; locum sibi

360 velle liberum praeberier, ubi nequam faciat.

nos hominem ad te adduximus.

LY. Itane ille est cupiens? **ADV.** Aurum habet. **LY.** Praeda haec meast.

ADV. Potare, amare vult. **LY.** Locum lepidum dabo.

ADV. At enim hic clam, furtim esse vult, ne quis sciat

365 neve arbiter sit. nam hic latro in Fayettevilla, Forti Braggi fuit.

CO. Nimis lepide de latrone, de Fayettevilla, Forti Braggi optume.

LY. Di deaeque vobis multa bona dent, cum mihi

et bene praecipitis et bonam praedam datis.

ADV. trecentos nummos Philippos portat praesidi.

370 **rex sum, si…adlexero:** *adlicio, -ere, -exi, -ectus,* "to entice," "to lure." In his excitement Lycus counts his chickens before they've hatched, by using a present tense verb in a future condition: "I am a king (i.e., 'I've hit the jackpot'), if I *will have* enticed…"

371 **tibi:** dative of advantage: "for you."
palumbem: *palumbes, -is,* m., "pigeon," "sucker." Here both meanings are present.
aream: *area, -ae,* f., "an open space"; here, a clearing where a hunter sets his traps.
usque: "all the way."

372 **meliust:** = *melius est,* which introduces the phrase *te illum… capere.*

373 **quid quod:** "What (about) *that which…*?" The *advocati* have not overtly introduced Collybisca to Lycus, so she pretends to be confused.

375 **illic:** = *ille,* just as *illoc* = *illo* in line 374. Both refer to Lycus.
ad istas res: "for those things."
probus: *probus, -a, -um,* "good," "competent." Note *probus* was Milphio's word for Collybisca too when introducing her onstage at line 310.
quaeritas: *quaerito, -are,* "to keep seeking," "to continue to search for"; a frequentative form of *quaero, -ere,* emphasizing Collybisca's repeated efforts to find some fun.

376 **vellem:** an imperfect potential subjunctive, used because Collybisca apparently thinks her wish will no longer be carried out. She worries that the *advocati* are abandoning her as they move off to the side. "I would like you to be watching when I give him the gold (but you probably won't)."
darem: attracted into this mood and tense by *vellem.*

377 **illinc:** "from that place." The *advocati* turn back to Collybisca and point to the place from which they will be watching.

378 **bonam dedistis mihi operam:** "You've looked after me well."

379 "That (the *lucrum*) at any rate (is going) in the direction in which an ass kicks with its heels." This is rather obscure. It seems that Lycus' loot is not coming to him but going nowhere, with the added notion of him getting kicked. Compare our phrase "to go to pot" (which originally had the sense of getting cut up to be cooked).

384 **ne:** "indeed."

385–387 **siquidem potes esse te pati…complexum contrectare:** *potes* introduces the infinitive *pati,* which in turn governs the accusative *te* and infinitive *esse* and the infinitive *contrectare. complexum* (which agrees with *te*) is from the deponent *complector* and so can have an active meaning: "If you are able to put up with (*pati*) being in a lovely place…fondling a lovely woman whom you've embraced." Lycus uses understatement ("if you can endure") to entice Collybisca.

387 **Is, leno, viam:** *viam* is an internal accusative: "You're going (i.e., leading) the way."

388 We have added the names of modern wines to get the point across. Plautus' wines were *Leucadio, Lesbio, Thasio,* and *Chio,* all named from Greek islands.

389 **vetustate vino edentulo:** "wine toothless with age. "

390 **latrocinantur:** *latrocinor, -ari,* "to serve as a mercenary soldier." Everything Lycus offers is mercenary, because, as he explains in the next line, it requires immediate payment in gold (*aurum…praesentarium*).

392 **quam ego dare:** Supply *malo.*

393 **evocemus:** deliberative subjunctive: "What if we call Agorastocles out?"

394 **egredere:** imperative.

395 **tute:** intensive form of *tu.*
inspectes: is in a purpose clause, and introduces an indirect statement with *dari.*

370 LY. Rex sum, si ego illum hodie ad me hominem adlexero!

ADV. Nos tibi palumbem ad aream usque adduximus:

nunc te illum meliust capere, si captum esse vis.

CO. Iamne itis? quid quod vobis mandavi, hospites?

ADV. Cum illoc te meliust tuam rem, adulescens, loqui:

375 illic est ad istas res probus quas quaeritas.

CO. Videre equidem vos vellem cum huic aurum darem.

ADV. Illinc procul nos istuc inspectabimus.

CO. Bonam dedistis mihi operam. LY. It ad me lucrum.

CO. Illud quidem quorsum asinus caedit calcibus.

380 LY. Blande hominem compellabo. hospes hospitem

salutat. salvum te advenire gaudeo.

CO. Multa tibi di dent bona …

LY. Hospitium te aiunt quaeritare. CO. Quaerito.

LY. Edepol ne tibi illud possum festivum dare,

385 siquidem potes esse te pati in lepido loco,

in lecto lepide strato lepidam mulierem

complexum contrectare. CO. Is, leno, viam.

LY. Ibi tu Leucadio, Chio, Gallo, Andre, Martini Rossique, Riunite …

vetustate vino edentulo aetatem inriges.

390 sed haec latrocinantur quae ego dixi omnia.

CO. Quid ita? LY. Quia aurum poscunt praesentarium.

CO. Quin hercle accipere tu non mavis quam ego dare.

ADV. Quid si evocemus huc foras Agorastoclem?

heus tu, qui furem captas, egredere ocius,

395 ut tute inspectes aurum lenoni dari.

3.4

397 **alteram dexteram:** This is our joke, we confess, but it's not unPlautine in spirit.

398 **sis:** = *si vis*, "if you will," i.e., "please." *hoc, hic,* and *hinc* all refer to the moneybag that Collybisca now gives to Lycus.

399 **Philippei:** See note at line 25.

403 A more easily understood word order would be *ibi alia quae reliqua fabulabimur.*

404 **castra Lejeuna:** Camp LeJeune, the second most famous military base in North Carolina. Collybisca forgot at which base she was supposed to say she was stationed (Ft. Bragg, see line 365), and came up with another. Plautus originally promised talk of *res Spartiaticas,* "affairs at Sparta."

405 **servum tenes:** Lycus interprets this as "*your* (i.e., Lycus') slave," thinking that the soldier is so lustful as to say, "I'm in your hands now, pimp." Collybisca knows that the *advocati* (and the audience) will interpret her remark as "Agorastocles' slave," further incriminating Lycus. Notice that Lycus and Collybisca exit on this line into Lycus' house. Such an exit in the middle of a scene is not unheard of but it is unusual.

406 **quid nunc mi[hi] auctores estis:** "What do you advise me (to do) now?"
   ut frugi sis: "That you do the right thing."

407 **animus:** "spirit, "courage." Agorastocles worries that he is not up to confronting Lycus.
   esto: second person future imperative: "Be as it allows (you to be)," "Do what you can."

410 **rem adversus populi saepe leges:** This is obscure. Somehow (the text, especially *saepe*, may be corrupt) it means: "(This is) a matter often against the laws of the people?" i.e., "This is generally illegal?"

411 **commeminisse:** treat as a present infinitive in sense, although pluperfect in form.

412 **ad praetorem:** "before the judge," the *praetor* being a judicial officer at Rome. Though Plautus sets his plays in Greece, they are populated by characters and circumstances that are often recognizably Roman.
   cum usus veniet: "when the need arises." *cum* with the future indicative is almost equivalent to *si,* "if."

413 **recenti re:** an ablative absolute: "the affair (Lycus' theft) being recent."
   aedis: accusative plural, used often for a single house (of several rooms).
   censeo: "I think you should."

414 **panem frangito:** a miserable pun as the *advocati* misunderstand, or pretend to misunderstand, *pultem* (the present subjunctive of *pulto, -are*) as the accusative singular of *puls, pultis,* f., "porridge." *frangito* is a future imperative. Agorastocles means, "If I knock, (and) he doesn't answer?" but this sounds just like "If he doesn't open his porridge?" The *advocati* reply: "Let him crunch (or break up) some bread."

415 **censen:** = *censesne,* "Do you think that…?" a question followed by subjunctive *interrogem,* followed by an indirect question with *veneritne.* So these two lines would read: "Do you think I should ask the man whether my slave has come to him (or his place)."

416 **mea serva:** Since Agorastocles is talking about springing the trap on Lycus, he refers to Collybisca as her real female self, as he will expect the *advocati* to do in their testimony.
   quippini: Starting here we added a few more *quippini*'s in order to make the annoying tone of the *advocati* even more apparent.

418 **furti:** *furtum, -i,* n., "theft." "He'll make himself an accessory to (implicate himself in) the theft."

3.4 [original lines 711–745, with cuts]

Collybisca hands over the money to Lycus, who takes her into his house. Agorastocles is there to see it all, and he checks to make sure that his witnesses observed the pimp's actions. Suddenly they see the pimp coming back out of the house and the witnesses put on disguises.

AG. Quid est? quid vultis, testes? **ADV.** Specta ad dexteram.

alteram dexteram! tua serva aurum ipsi lenoni dabit.

CO. Age, accipe hoc sis: hic sunt numerati aurei

trecenti nummi, qui vocantur Philippei.

400   hinc me procura; propere hosce apsumi volo.

LY. Edepol fecisti prodigum promum tibi.

age, eamus intro. **CO.** Te sequor. **LY.** Age, age, ambula,

ibi quae reliqua alia fabulabimur.

CO. Eadem narrabo tibi castra Lejeuna.

405   **LY.** Quin sequere me ergo. **CO.** Abduc intro. servum tenes …

AG. Quid nunc mi auctores estis? **ADV.** Vt frugi sis.

AG. Quid si animus esse non sinit? **ADV.** Esto ut sinit.

AG. Vidistis leno cum aurum accepit? **ADV.** Vidimus.

AG. Eam vos meam esse servam scitis? **ADV.** Scivimus.

410   **AG.** Rem adversus populi saepe leges? **ADV.** Scivimus.

AG. Em istaec volo ergo vos commeminisse omnia,

mox ad praetorem cum usus veniet. **ADV.** Meminimus.

AG. Quid si recenti re aedis pultem? **ADV.** Censeo.

AG. Si pultem, non recludet? **ADV.** Panem frangito.

415   **AG.** Si exierit leno, censen hominem interrogem,

mea serva ad eum veneritne? **ADV.** Quippini?

AG. Extemplo denegabit. **ADV.** Iuratus quidem. Quippini?

AG. Homo furti sese adstringet … **ADV.** Hau dubium id quidemst. Quippini?

AG. At dico .. immo vero .. iam tandem .. **ADV.** Quippini? Quippini…

420 **Diespiter vos perduit:** In classical Latin this would be *Iuppiter vos perdat*.

422 **tacendi:** genitive of the gerund: "It's time for being quiet."

423 **egredier:** an archaic passive infinitive (= *egrediri*).

424–425 **si voles operire capita:** "If you'd like to cover our heads, [go ahead and do so]." *voles* is future tense. This is a costuming stage direction called for directly in the text.

426 **illi:** Lycus. The dative goes with *inlices*, "... us, who were the enticers for him of such an evil affair," i.e., "who enticed him into such an unfortunate business."

3.5

429 **portendier:** another archaic present passive infintive (= *portendi*).

430 **eis explicavi meam rem...lucro:** "I've expanded my livelihood with wealth from these (i.e., the gold from Collybisca)." *lucro* is an ablative of respect.

432 Supply the infinitive *valere* after each *volo*.

433 **verum non tibi:** "But not for you." In Lycus' opinion the girls' welfare should not matter to Agorastocles, since the young man is never going to get his hands on them.

434 **si audes:** "If you please." *audeo* can mean "to intend" in early Latin.

436 Lycus lamely jokes that Agorastocles' lunch must have been awfully hot, since the only thing he's accomplishing by asking for Adelphasium is to cool off his mouth.

438 **hoc age:** an idiomatic call to attention, stronger than *age* alone.

439 **factum:** = *factum esse*.

440 **mentire:** = *mentiris*, from *mentior, -iri*, "to lie."

441 **quibus:** dative, with the antecedent unexpressed: "Thus it has been reported to me *by people* (unexpressed *ab eis*) in whom (*quibus*) I trust."

442 **captatum:** a supine, expressing purpose (see the note on *habitu*, line 77).

443 **nec quicquam tui:** "nor anything of yours"; *tui*, genitive of *tuus*, used substantively.

444 **mementote:** future imperative, second person plural. The future imperative of this verb is often used with no difference in meaning from a present imperative.

420   **AG.** Diespiter vos perduit! **ADV.** Te quippini?

       AG. Ibo et pultabo ianuam. **ADV.** Ita, quippini?

       AG. Tacendi tempus est, nam crepuerunt fores.

       foras egredier video lenonem Lycum.

       adeste quaeso. **ADV.** Quippini? si voles

425   operire capita, ne nos leno noverit,

       qui illi malae rei tantae fuimus inlices.

3.5 [original lines 746–795, with cuts]

Agorastocles confronts Lycus, accusing him of theft. Lycus recognizes the witnesses through their disguises, but when they reveal that Collybisca really is Agorastocles' slave, Lycus realizes that he is ruined. Agorastocles gets his money back, but he inexplicably lets Lycus get away for now.

       LY. Suspendant omnes nunciam se haruspices

       qui in re divina dudum dicebant mihi

       malum damnumque maximum portendier:

430   eis explicavi meam rem postilla lucro!

       AG. Salvus sis, leno. **LY.** Di te ament, Agorastocles.

       AG. Valeant apud te quos volo; atque hau te volo.

       LY. Valent ut postulatumst, verum non tibi.

       AG. Mitte ad me, si audes, hodie Adelphasium tuam,

435   die festo celebri nobilique Aphrodisiis.

       LY. Calidum prandisti prandium hodie? dic mihi.

       AG. Quid iam? **LY.** Quia os nunc frigefactas, cum rogas.

       AG. Hoc age sis, leno. servam esse audivi meam

       apud te. **LY.** Apud me? numquam factum reperies.

440   **AG.** Mentire. nam ad te venit aurumque attulit;

       ita mihi renuntiatumst, quibus credo satis.

       LY. Malus es, captatum me advenis cum testibus.

       tuorum apud me nemost nec quicquam tui.

       AG. Mementote illud, advocati. **ADV.** Meminimus.

445 **teneo:** This refers to grasping with the mind, like our "I've got it!"
    quid sit: an indirect question.

446 **Fayettevillianum:** "from Fayetteville." See the note on line 365 for explanation.

447–448 **id nunc his...facturum lucri:** a complex construction. *id*, an internal accusative, refers to the indirect statement in the next line; *his* is a dative of disadvantage: "The brain is now burning to them (i.e., *their* brain) regarding this (*id*), that I am going to make 300 bucks profit," i.e., "They are now seething mad about my making 300 bucks."

449–450 Easier word order might be *nunc hunc, quia inimicum esse mihi sciverunt, eum adlegarunt.* Both *hunc* and *eum* refer to Agorastocles.

449 **mihi:** dative with *inimicum.*

450 **adlegarunt:** the shortened form of *adlegaverunt.*
    qui servum diceret: relative purpose clause.

451 **compositast:** = *composita est.*

452 **eo:** an ablative of separation, referring to the gold.

453 **lupo:** dative of separation with *eripere.* "Lycus" means "wolf" in Greek, and Lycus is proud of it.
    nugas agunt: "They're working on foolish stuff," i.e., "They're wasting their time."

454 **istast:** = *ista est.*
    vilica: The *advocati* no longer need to hide Collybisca's gender, so they speak of her as feminine as Agorastocles had recently instructed them at line 416.

455 **Fayettevilliatem:** "a Fayettevillian"; agrees with *quam*; originally *Spartiatem* in Plautus. See the note on line 365 for an explanation of the reference to Fayetteville, North Carolina.

456 **idque:** *id* goes with *aurum.* "That gold," i.e., the gold we've been talking about.
    adeo: adds a further point: "what's more."

457 **vae vestrae aetati:** *vae* means "alas" when one says it about oneself, and can be used to curse someone else with similar misfortune; *aetas* here means "life," thus "Bad luck on your life," i.e., "Bad luck to you."
    in mundo est tuae: Supply *aetati* with *tuae*; *in mundo* means "in readiness for."

458 **furcifer:** a term of abuse, from *furca, -ae,* f., "fork," a forked wooden frame fastened as punishment to one's arms, and *fero, ferre,* "to carry"; thus, "fork-carrier," "wretch!"

459 **operam date:** "pay attention"; Agorastocles wants to make sure that the *advocati* can provide good testimony against Lycus in court.

462 **cum ego habui:** The *cum*-clause explains Lycus' emotional exclamation *eheu:* "Alas, since I had ..."; Plautus often uses the indicative in *cum*-clauses.
    hariolos haruspices: "legitimate soothsayers." Lycus must finally admit that the *haruspices* at whom he railed as worthless forecasters earlier (lines 228–231) were correct in their reading of misfortune in his future.

464 **id quod mali:** *mali* is a partitive genitive with *id quod:* "that bit of evil which," or in better English, "whatever evil." The evil they promise takes immediate effect.

465 **consulam:** future of *consulo, -ere,* "consult," "ask."
    quo...modo: "how," introducing an indirect question.

466 **censeant:** a subjunctive in an indirect question, introducing an indirect statement (*aequum esse* with the *esse* left out). Lycus' friends are the subject of *censeant.*
    potissimum: "in the best way."

445 LY. Hahahae! iam teneo quid sit, perspexi modo.

hi qui illum dudum conciliaverunt mihi

peregrinum Fayettevillianum, id nunc his cerebrum uritur,

me esse hos trecentos Philippos facturum lucri.

nunc hunc, inimicum quia esse sciverunt mihi,

450 eum adlegarunt suum qui servum diceret

cum auro esse apud me. compositast fallacia

ut eo me privent atque inter se dividant.

lupo agnum eripere postulant. nugas agunt.

ADV. Periisti, leno! nam istast huius vilica

455 quam tibi nos esse Fayettevilliatem diximus,

idque in istoc adeo aurum inest marsuppio.

LY. Vae vostrae aetati! ADV. Id quidem in mundo est tuae.

AG. Age omitte actutum, furcifer, marsuppium:

manifesto fur es. mihi quaeso hercle operam date,

460 dum me videatis servam ab hoc abducere.

LY. Nunc pol ego perii certo, haud arbitrario.

eheu, cum ego habui hariolos haruspices!

qui si quid bene promittunt, perspisso evenit,

id quod mali promittunt, praesentarium est.

465 nunc ibo, amicos consulam quo me modo

suspendere aequum censeant potissimum.

3.6

467 **age tu progredere:** *age* is often joined with another imperative (*progredere*) and means "Come on, get going!" Agorastocles is speaking to Collybisca.

istinc: "from that place," i.e., from Lycus' house.

467–468 **quid nunc, sceleste leno:** Agorastocles thinks Lycus is still onstage, although the pimp has somehow managed to slip away. As it turns out, Plautus will let Lycus escape from this trap so he can be trapped again in the second half of the play.

468 **utinam...abierit:** a perfect subjunctive used for a wish that something may prove to have happened: "I hope that he's gone..." For *malam crucem*, see the note on line 105.

469 **numquid me:** Supply *vis*: "Do you want *me* (to do) anything (else)?"

sumas ornatum tuum: "Put on your (regular) clothes (and take off that soldier's costume)."

470 **bonam dedistis...operam:** "You've been very helpful."

471 **in comitio estote obviam:** "Be at hand in court," i.e., "meet me in court" in order to testify on Agorastocles' behalf at the trial of Lycus. *estote* is the second-person plural future imperative of *sum*.

473 **iniuriam...insignite postulat:** apparently a joke, since *postulo*, which can be used for everyday demands, was frequently used in legal contexts to mean "prosecute." Agorastocles "persecutes" the *advocati* by not giving them any reward for all their help.

474 **isti nostri:** *isti* shows their contempt for the rich: "This is the way these rich boys of ours are."

475 **si quid bene facias:** "if you do them any favor." *quid* (= *aliquid*). *si* introduces a mixed condition, with a future less vivid protasis (*facias*, present subjunctive), but a present general apodosis (*est*). The *advocati* view doing a rich man a favor as a somewhat distant prospect, but want to stress the fact that his gratitude will be paltry.

pluma: ablative of comparison with *levior*.

476 **si quid peccatumst:** the impersonal construction of the verb *peccare*, in the perfect tense: "If any mistake has been made." *peccatumst* (= *peccatum est*). The *advocati* don't want to say that they might make a mistake.

plumbeas: "leaden," i.e., "heavy," "oppressive."

iras gerunt: "they harbor anger (in their hearts)."

477 **abeamus:** hortatory subjunctive (jussive in the first person): "Let us go..."

domos: with a verb of motion (*abeamus*), this needs no preposition (*ad* or *in*).

sultis: = *si vultis*; this is the plural form of *sis* (= *si vis*), "please."

(See a discussion of the *advocati* and the role of Act 3 in the play in the director's note at the end of 3.6.)

4.1 & 4.2

478 **macerat:** *macero, -are*, "to vex."

479 **amanti:** "to one who is in love." *servire*, "to be a slave (to someone)," is the subject and takes the dative case (*amanti*).

quod amat: this phrase functions as the object of *caret*. The antecedent of *qui* is *amanti*.

480 **recipere...se:** "to bring oneself back," "to return"; this verb is the subject of an indirect statement.

481 **eunuchum:** We, not Plautus, made Syncerastus a eunuch. See the director's notes for further explanation.

quid habeat sermonis: "what he says." *sermonis* is a partitive genitive after *quid*.

482 **alter...gentium:** "any other person on earth."

483 **caeno conlitus:** "made foul by filth."

484 **corruptelae:** from *corruptela, -ae*, f., "enticement," "source of seduction."

di vostram (= *vestram*) **fidem:** a common idiom, "Ye gods! (I beg) your faith!" It occurs again at line 523.

3.6 [original lines 796–816, with cuts]

Agorastocles thanks the witnesses and asks them to appear in court on the following day.

AG. Age tu progredere, ut testes videant te ire istinc foras. Quid nunc,

sceleste leno? **ADV.** Abscessit. **AG.** Vtinam hinc abierit malam crucem.

CO. Numquid me? **AG.** Abscedas, sumas ornatum tuum.

470   bonam dedistis, advocati, operam mihi.

cras mane, quaeso, in comitio estote obviam.

vos valete. **ADV.** Et tu vale.

iniuriam illic insignite postulat:

verum ita sunt isti nostri divites:

475   si quid bene facias, levior pluma est gratia;

si quid peccatumst, plumbeas iras gerunt.

domos abeamus nostras, sultis, nunciam.

4.1 [original lines 817–822, with cuts]

Milphio returns and spots Syncerastus, the pimp's eunuch, approaching.

MI. Studeo hunc lenonem perdere qui meum erum miserum macerat.

servire amanti miseria est, praesertim qui quod amat caret.

480   attat! e fano recipere video se Syncerastum,

lenonis eunuchum; quid habeat sermonis auscultabo.

4.2 [original lines 823–929, with cuts]

Syncerastus complains about the unpleasant company his master keeps. Milphio and Syncerastus engage in some good-natured banter and then Syncerastus reveals a secret about his much hated master: Lycus bought Adelphasium and Anterastilis, although he knew they were freeborn citizens of Carthage. Romans exacted heavy penalties for a dealer in freeborn people, and Milphio realizes that Agorastocles could prosecute Lycus and get Adelphasium in the bargain.

SYNCERASTUS. Neque peiiurior neque peior alter usquam est gentium

quam erus meus est, neque tam luteus neque tam caeno conlitus.

quae illic hominum corruptelae fiunt! di vostram fidem!

485   **Acheruntem:** *Acheruns, Acheruntis,* m., "the underworld."

486   **equitem…fugitivum:** Syncerastus lists in descending social rank the low types that come to Lycus' brothel. *Equites* were wealthy men who could afford the expense of outfitting their own horses for the cavalry. *Pedites* were the infantry. *Libertini* (freedmen) were former slaves or descendants of slaves, like the *advocati* (see Act 3.1). At the end of the list are the worst, the *fugitivi* (runaway slaves) and *fures* (thieves). Note that Syncerastus is admitting that Lycus regularly takes in runaway slaves, which is exactly the type of legal trap that Agorastocles and Milphio have set for the pimp.

488   **tenebrae latebrae, bibitur estur:** In each pair of words, Syncerastus omits the connective (*et* or *atque*). *tenebrae* and *latebrae* indicate, literally and figuratively, that Lycus' place is a really "shady joint." *bibitur* and *estur* are impersonal passives (from *bibo, -ere* and *edo, -ere*) that emphasize actions without specifying the actors: "there's eating and drinking," "people eat and drink."

489   **lubet:** = *libet,* "it's a pleasure to…," "I'd like to…" followed by an infinitive.

   lubens: = *libens,* present participle of *libet,* "pleased," "willing." Translate as an adverb ("willingly"), or (with *ausculto*) "I'm happy to listen."

490   **cum hic:** *cum* here with the indicative means "whenever"; *hic,* "here."

491   **domum:** Compare the use of *domos* in line 477.

   hostiis: ablative of means.

493   **lepidam Venerem:** Exclamations often appear in the accusative case.

494   **placavere:** = *placaverunt.*

   denuo: "again," "for a second time."

495   **qui:** = *quis.*

496   **amice facis:** With adverbs (*amice*), forms of *facere* can mean "to act."

498   **habe rem pactam:** "regard the matter as agreed upon," "count on it," "consider it done."

   futurumst: = *futurum est.* The subject of this clause would appear to be Milphio's intention to help Syncerastus at some future point.

499   **mihi vapulandum sit:** "I must be beaten." *vapulo, -are* means "to be beaten" in *active* forms; so the impersonal form of the passive periphrastic must be used, and *mihi* here is a dative of disadvantage, not of agent.

500   **quid viri:** "what sort of man."

   sis: second-person singular, present tense, active voice, subjunctive mood of the verb *esse.* Supply the word *malus* to complete the thought: "May you be bad to yourself."

501   **appone:** supply *onus* as the subject.

503   **refero vasa salva:** In the previous line Syncerastus claimed that he was doing something that adulterers rarely did. This punch line plays on two meanings of the word *vasa.* It could refer to containers, such as Lycus had used at his sacrifices, or to male genitals. In ancient Rome an aggrieved husband could punish his wife and adulterer on the spot if he caught them in the act. Thus an adulterer might not make it home with all his "equipment" intact.

   perduint: an ancient form of the subjunctive *perdant.*

505   **mihi:** "for myself."

   cedo: This is not from the verb *cedere,* "to yield," but is instead an imperative that means "give"; here, "Out with it!"

506   **Diespiter:** = *Iuppiter.*

508   **facilest:** = *facile est.*

508–510   Syncerastus says that he doesn't have the wings to fly (i.e., doesn't have the courage or strength to trick his master). Milphio crudely suggests that Syncerastus' armpit hair could in sixty days grow long enough to allow him to fly. *hirquinae* and *volucres* modify *alae:* "your goatish (i.e., smelly), swift wings."

485 quodvis genus ibi hominum videas, quasi Acheruntem veneris,

equitem, peditem, libertinum, furem an fugitivum velis,

omnia genera recipiuntur; itaque in totis aedibus

tenebrae latebrae, bibitur, estur quasi in popina, hau secus.

MI. Adire lubet hominem et autem nimis eum ausculto lubens.

490 SY. Haec cum hic video fieri, crucior.

nunc domum haec ab aede Veneris refero vasa, ubi hostiis

erus nequivit propitiare Venerem suo festo die.

MI. Lepidam Venerem! SY. Nam meretrices nostrae primis hostiis

Venerem placavere extemplo. MI. O lepidam Venerem denuo!

495 SY. Nunc domum ibo. MI. Heus, Synceraste! SY. Syncerastum qui vocat?

MI. Tuus amicus. SY. Haud amice facis qui cum onere offers moram.

MI. At ob hanc moram tibi reddam operam ubi voles, ubi iusseris.

habe rem pactam. SY. Si futurumst, do tibi operam hanc. MI. Quo modo?

SY. Vt enim ubi mihi vapulandum sit, tu corium sufferas.

500 apage, nescio quid viri sis. MI. Malus sum. SY. Tibi sis. MI. Te volo.

SY. At onus urget. MI. At tu appone et respice ad me. quid agis?

SY. Facio quod manufesti moechi hau ferme solent.

MI. Quid id est? SY. Refero vasa salva. MI. Di te et tuum erum perduint!

SY. Me non perdent; meum erum ut perdant facere possum, si velim,

505 ni mihi metuam, Milphio. MI. Quid id est? cedo.

SY. Diespiter me sic amabit ... MI. Vt quidem edepol dignus es.

SY. Vt ego hanc familiam interire cupio. MI. Adde operam, si cupis.

SY. Sine pinnis volare hau facilest: meae alae pinnas non habent.

MI. Nolito edepol devellisse: iam his duobus mensibus

510 **i in malam rem:** a common insult, also used at line 118.

i tu atque erus: Although this sentence has a plural subject, a speaker will often have in mind only the subject closest to the verb, and thus Milphio uses a singular imperative.

511 **animum inducam:** *inducere animum*, "to lead one's mind," "to bring oneself to…"

512 **meo periclo:** "at my own risk."

male: can mean "ill-advisedly."

515 **Crurifragium:** "Mr. Legsbashed." Syncerastus makes up a humorous name out of the roots of the words for "leg" (*crus, cruris,* n.) and "to break" (*frango, -ere, fregi, fractum*).

516 **fide non melius creditur:** "Faith is the best basis for trust." *creditur* is an impersonal passive ("there is trust," "people believe"), and *fide* is an ablative of comparison. With this silly maxim, Milphio tries to persuade Syncerastus to put his trust in him and divulge his secret about the pimp.

517 **loquere:** singular imperative.

518 **ingenuast:** = *ingenua est.*

519 **soror illius altera Anterastilis:** "the sister of that one (Adelphasium), the other girl, Anterastilis." We should supply *ingenua est* to complete the meaning of this line.

520 **cedo qui:** "Tell (me) how…" For *cedo*, see the note on line 505.

emit: The subject is Lycus, the tense is perfect. *emo, emere, emi, emptum,* "to buy." The purchase and sale of freeborn women (*ingenuae*) was illegal in Roman society.

Anactorio: *Anactorium, -ii,* n., a port city in western Greece near Calydon.

parvolas: = *parvulas,* "when they were very young."

521 **praedone Siculo:** *praedo, praedonis,* m., "pirate"; *Siculus, -a, -um,* "Sicilian."

Giddenenem nutricem: Next to their parents, the nurse who fed and cared for young children of affluent families would be the closest thing they had to a relative. These slaves served originally as wet nurses (surrogate breast feeders) and nannies, but later in the children's lives became guardians, tutors, confidants, and assistants in other ways.

522 **furtivas:** *furtivus, -a, -um,* "stolen."

523 **Carthagine:** ablative of origin.

di vostram (= *vestram*) **fidem!:** See the note for line 484.

524–526 Milphio remarks with comic surprise that Agorastocles was also stolen from Carthage at a young age. Nowhere are such kidnappings as common and coincidental as in Roman comedy.

525 **gnatust:** = *gnatus est.*

526 **qui:** "the one who," referring to the pirate who stole Agorastocles (*eum* both times in this line). Agorastocles was, at this time, sold to Milphio's original master Antidamas. Agorastocles eventually gained his freedom, became Antidamas' adopted son and heir, and obtained Milphio as his slave.

527 **quo:** Purpose clauses containing comparatives (such as *facilius*) are introduced by *quo* rather than *ut.*

527–528 *adserere manu* means to lay a hand upon someone to claim them, and with *liberali causa* it means "to claim someone as free." The fact that the girls and Agorastocles are from Carthage is another reason why Agorastocles should prosecute the pimp and claim the girls as free.

528 **popularis:** = *populares.*

ad incitas lenonem rediget: an idiom taken from a Roman board game; our parallel is "He will drive the pimp into checkmate."

529 **faxint:** = *fecerint.* The perfect subjunctive is sometimes used in wishes: "May the gods accomplish…"

510 volucres tibi erunt tuae hirquinae. **SY.** I in malam rem! **MI.** I tu atque erus.

SY. Animum inducam facile ut tibi istuc credam, ni te noverim.

MI. Crede audacter meo periclo. **SY.** Male credam et credam tamen.

At ego hoc metuo, Milphio.

si erus meus me esse elocutum cuiquam mortali sciat,

515 continuo is me ex Syncerasto Crurifragium fecerit.

MI. Fide non melius creditur.

loquere (locus occasioque est) libere: hic soli sumus.

SY. Adelphasium, quam erus deamat tuus, ingenuast. **MI.** Quo modo?

SY. Eodem quo soror illius altera Anterastilis.

520 **MI.** Cedo qui id credam. **SY.** Quia illas emit in Anactorio parvolas

de praedone Siculo, duas illas et Giddenenem nutricem earum tertiam.

et ille qui eas vendebat dixit se furtivas vendere:

ingenuas Carthagine aibat esse. **MI.** Di vostram fidem!

nimium lepidum memoras facinus. nam erus meus, Agorastocles,

525 ibidem gnatust, inde surruptus fere sexennis, postibi

qui eum surrupuit huc devexit meoque ero eum hic vendidit.

SY. Omnia memoras quo id facilius fiat: manu eas adserat, suas

popularis, liberali causa. profecto ad incitas lenonem rediget, si eas abduxerit.

ita di faxint ne apud lenonem hunc serviam!

530 **qui:** The antecedent is Syncerastus.

faxo: an alternative form for *fecero*, the future perfect tense, indicative mood. Usually we would expect in this construction that *ut* + subjunctive would follow the verb *facere* ("I will have made it that…") but here we just get a simple future indicative, *eris*.

531 **numquid aliud me morare, Milphio:** *morare* = *moraris*. *numquid* functions as an adverbial accusative: "Do you detain me for some other reason, Milphio?"

532 **tuost:** = *tuo est*.

ero in manu: We use much the same idiom (in the plural) in English. "I'm in your hands now" (i.e., the situation is under your control and responsibility).

533 **cura:** an imperative from *curo, -are*, "to take care," "to make sure."

clanculum: This adverb modifies the verb *sint dicta*.

dictumst: = *dictum est*.

535 **illic hinc abiit:** Milphio now speaks to the audience. *illic* (= *ille*), i.e., Syncerastus.

536 **exiti:** partitive genitive dependent on *tantum*; together they mean "so much destruction."

537 **haec:** Although outside the *ut* clause, this word is the object of the verb *memorem*.

ero: not a verb as in 533, but the dative of *erus, -i*, m., "master," as in 526.

5.1

Note: In the available manuscripts of this play, Hanno is here given a lot of gibberish that's supposed to be Punic, and may once have been Punic before generations of scribes—who naturally knew no Punic— garbled it beyond repair. We changed the "Punic" lines in Plautus' original text of this act (Plautus' lines 930–949, and all subsequent occurrences) into English. Our theatrical reasons for this change are found in the director's notes for Act 5. The "Punic" lines are recorded in the appendix that appears after the Text & Commentary. Our replacement for these lines is ad-libbed monologue recorded only on the videotape.

538 **veneror:** Hanno is the essence of piety, and so he begins with a prayer to the local gods. With *veneror*, those to whom one prays are in the accusative, and the things for which one prays are expressed by *ut* + subjunctive.

540 Hanno first prays that the gods sanction his arrival in Calydon. It was always important to follow the correct religious procedures and the adverb *rite* means "with all due consideration of the proper rites." Literally, Hanno says, "I pray that, inasmuch as (*quod*) I have come here on my own business, I have come *rite*."

541 **measque hic ut gnatas:** the *-que* joins the second part of Hanno's prayer, which is introduced by *ut*.

hic: "here."

gnatas: = *natas* (i.e., *filias*).

542 **siritis:** = *siveritis*, perfect subjunctive of *sino, -ere, si(v)i, situm*, "to allow." The perfect subjunctive occasionally appears where we would expect the present tense.

di vostram (= *vestram*) **fidem:** As we saw at line 484, this is a common idiomatic exclamation: "ye gods! (I beg) your faith!"

543 Hanno has finished his prayer and he now tells the audience his reason for coming to Calydon.

544 **sibi quod faciundum fuit:** i.e., he died. *faciundum* (= *faciendum*) *fuit* is a passive periphrastic (future passive participle + a form of *esse*) referring to past time (*fuit*). The subject of *aiunt* and *praedicant* is a general "they," i.e., the people of Calydon.

546 **hospitalem hanc tesseram:** In antiquity, when friends parted for a long time, they broke a token or amulet (*tessera*) in half, and each kept one half, so that at their reunion they might know each other by comparing the halves. Here Hanno shows the audience his half of the token. Agorastocles will produce his own half at line 621.

548 **hos percontabor:** Hanno notices Agorastocles and Milphio (*hos*) coming outdoors.

530 MI. Hercle qui meus conlibertus faxo eris, si di volent.

SY. Ita di faxint. numquid aliud me morare, Milphio?

MI. Valeas beneque ut tibi sit. SY. Pol istuc tibi et tuost ero in manu.

vale et haec cura clanculum ut sint dicta. MI. Non dictumst. vale.

mihi commoditatem creas.

535 illic hinc abiit. di immortales meum erum servatum volunt

et hunc disperditum lenonem: tantum eum instat exiti.

ibo intro haec ut meo ero memorem.

5.1 [original lines 930–960, with cuts]

We are introduced to the Carthaginian Hanno who has spent many years in search of his lost daughters. He is particularly hopeful that he may receive some help here in Calydon since he knows that an old friend of his, Antidamas, had lived here and left a son, Agorastocles, as his successor.

HANNO. Deos deasque veneror

qui hanc urbem colunt

540 ut quod de mea re huc veni rite venerim,

measque hic ut gnatas et mei fratris filium

reperire me siritis, di vostram fidem.

sed hic mihi antehac hospes Antidamas fuit;

eum fecisse aiunt sibi quod faciundum fuit.

545 eius filium esse hic praedicant Agorastoclem:

ad eum hospitalem hanc tesseram mecum fero;

is in hisce habitare monstratust regionibus.

hos percontabor qui hinc egrediuntur foras.

5.2

549 ain: = *aisne.*

  dixe: = *dixisse.*

551 frugi esse: "to do the right thing."

552 adseres...manu: *adserere manu* means "to lay a hand upon someone, to claim them," and with *liberali causa* it means "to claim someone as free"; see the note on lines 527–528.

557–558 sed quae illa avis est...circumductust pallio: Milphio has suddenly caught sight of Hanno and makes fun of his appearance. *tunicis* here clearly refers to the long undergarment worn by Roman women, not the shorter Roman male undergarment. The poet Ennius, a contemporary of Plautus, similarly refers to Carthaginian dress as effeminate (fragment 270). Milphio ridicules Hanno's long flowing garment with loose sleeves, a style of dress common among Carthaginians and people from other cultures, especially those from the Near East. The "bird" reference is a recognition of the loose, winglike sleeves of the garment.

  The *pallium* was a cloak worn as a traditional overgarment by Greek males. (Remember that this is supposed to be a Greek city inhabited by Greeks. Because of this wearing of the *pallium*, Roman comedies based on Greek originals were called *fabulae palliatae*.) Hanno, as a foreigner, would not be wearing a *pallium* over his long tunic, and Milphio assumes that this man must have had his *pallium* stolen at the bathhouse, a crime so common in the ancient world that it became a running joke.

558 circumductust: = *circumductus est.*

559 Punicast: = *Punica est.* Romans tended to call Carthaginians *Punici* when they meant to insult them. Throughout this act Milphio nearly always uses a form of *Punicus, -a,- um* to refer to Carthaginians, whereas other characters mix in the neutral *Carthaginiensis, -e* to describe a person from Carthage. The exception to this is that the Carthaginian language is called "Punic," without necessarily being derogatory. *Punici* became a common name for the people and culture of Carthage as a reference to Carthage's origin as a colony of the eastern Mediterranean kingdom of Phoenicia.

  guggast:= *gugga est.* We have no idea what *gugga* means, but given Milphio's abusive behavior towards Hanno throughout this scene, it must be insulting.

560–561 Milphio turns his jokes against Hanno's slaves: "They must be relics because they're all hunched over (like old people)," literally: "They're all laden down with packs on their backs," but the reference is clearly to their backs being bent with age.

561 qui: adverbial *qui*, "how."

562–563 Milphio quips that these Carthaginian slaves must not have fingers because they don't wear rings where they're supposed to (on their fingers). Instead they wear rings in their ears. Both Carthaginian men and women, like many in ancient Eastern cultures, might wear earrings. Western males, like Greeks and Romans, did not wear earrings.

565–566 Note the irony in Hanno's statement that if these men don't understand Punic, he will speak to them in their own language. Agorastocles and Milphio are Greeks, but the stage language they speak is Latin. This line plays off the facility Carthaginians seem to have had with using foreign languages, an ability that not all Greeks and Romans considered a positive quality in foreigners (see line 610).

567 ais: the verb *aio* usually means "to say yes" or "to speak," but with *quid* here and in line 572 you could translate it as "eh?" or "what do you say?"

  ecquid: "anything at all."

569 qui...perierim Carthagine: The verb in this relative clause is subjunctive because it provides the reason for Agorastocles' inability to speak Punic. "Since I disappeared from Carthage..."

5.2 [original lines 961–1119, with cuts]

*Milphio and Agorastocles enter discussing Syncerastus' revelations. When they catch sight of Hanno, Milphio offers to play the role of interpreter, though he really knows very little Punic (which is improvised as English in our version of the play). Milphio takes this opportunity to make fun of the foreigner, until Hanno unexpectedly begins speaking Latin. He and Agorastocles realize that they are uncle and nephew and Milphio is scolded offstage by Agorastocles for mocking his relative. Milphio returns to enlist Hanno's help in a new plot to catch Lycus based on the new information that he learned in Act 4. The trick will involve Hanno acting as if these two prostitutes are his long lost daughters in order to get them away from Lycus. Of course, they **are** Hanno's daughters, so we have the beginning of the end to the recognition scene.*

    AG. Ain tu tibi dixe Syncerastum, Milphio,

550 eas esse ingenuas ambas surrupticias

    Carthaginiensis? **MI.** Aio, et, si frugi esse vis,

    eas liberali iam adseres causa manu.

    HA. Pro di immortales, opsecro vostram fidem!

    quam orationem hanc aures dulcem devorant?

555 **AG.** Si ad eam rem testis habeam, faciam quod iubes.

    MI. Quid tu mihi testis? quin tu insistis fortiter?

    sed quae illa avis est quae huc cum tunicis advenit?

    numnam in balineis circumductust pallio?

    AG. Facies quidem edepol Punicast. **MI.** Guggast homo.

560 servos quidem edepol veteres antiquosque habet.

    AG. Qui scis? **MI.** Viden omnes sarcinatos consequi?

    atque ut opinor digitos in manibus non habent.

    AG. Quid iam? **MI.** Quia incedunt cum anulatis auribus.

    HA. Adibo hosce atque appellabo Punice.

565 si respondebunt, Punice pergam loqui;

    si non, tum ad horum mores linguam vertero.

    MI. Quid ais tu? ecquid commeministi Punice?

    AG. Nihil edepol. nam qui scire potui, dic mihi,

    qui illim sexennis perierim Carthagine?

570 **ad:** "in accordance with."

570–571 Hanno delivers these lines as an aside to the audience. He remarks seriously that children were often kidnapped from Carthage, but as we remarked above, these kidnappings are exceptionally common in comedies.

571 **periere:** = *perierunt.*

572 **vin:** = *visne.*

575 **quoiatis:** an interrogative adjective meaning "of what country."

576 **halo:** Milphio's version of "Hello." His knowledge of Hanno's language is limited. He can manage a greeting and understand an introduction, but for most of Hanno's lines Milphio makes up his translation based on the sounds in Hanno's speech. Plautus gave Hanno lines in some form of Punic (or something that would have sounded like Punic to the Roman ear), but in our adaptation of the play we changed Hanno's Punic to English for reasons that we explain in the director's notes to Act 5. (For Punic text of this and all following lines, see Appendix.) In each case of Milphio's mistranslation that follows, we wrote our own English line to match the sound of the words Milphio was confusing in the original play's "Punic." We <u>underline</u> in the notes below, the sounds that we made up to be the source of Milphio's mistranslations.

577 Baal was a principal Phoenician-Carthaginian god, mentioned often in the Bible as a god whose worship was very popular among other peoples who had contact with the Phoenicians.

580 **Mytthumbalis:** Latin genitive singular of Hanno's father's name, Mytthumbal. The *-bal* at the end of the name is reminiscent of the common Carthaginian suffix found in the names of famous Carthaginians like Hannibal and Hasdrubal. The ending is an honorific version of the name of their god, Baal. Even though in the original play, Milphio is probably translating Hanno accurately here by stating that Hanno said he was the son of Mytthumbal of Carthage, we decided to have Milphio misconstrue Hanno's words from the very beginning. So we made up the phrase "Mother of Baal" (line 577) to play off this name in Milphio's translation.

581 <u>**Don**</u>**'t know much Punic…:** Milphio will imagine that he hears the Latin word for gift (*donum, -i,* n.) in Hanno's opening "Don't…"

582 **doni…nescioquid:** A genitive is often used in conjunction with a neuter pronoun. This literally means "something of a gift" or in better English, "some gift."
audin: = *audisne.*
pollicitarier: an old-fashioned form of the passive infinitive, *pollicitari.*

585 <u>**maybe**</u> <u>**you**</u> <u>**could**</u> help <u>**me**</u>: Hanno strokes his beard while saying this line and so Milphio thinks that Hanno has come down with some disease of the mouth, *miseram…buccam* (line 586).

587 **arbitrarier:** an archaic passive infinitive (= *arbitrari*).

589 **numquid opus sit:** "what is necessary or needed."

589 Milphio's final jokes about Hanno's clothing. Carthaginian male garments flowed outward without restraint of a belt (*sona*), probably making them look even funnier to the Romans.

570 HA. Pro di immortales! plurumi ad illum modum

periere pueri liberi Carthagine.

MI. Quid ais tu? AG. Quid vis? MI. Vin appellem hunc Punice?

AG. An scis? MI. Nullus me est hodie Poenus Poenior.

AG. Adi atque appella, quid velit, quid venerit,

575 qui sit, quoiatis, unde sit: ne parseris.

MI. Halo. quoiates estis aut quo ex oppido?

HA. Mother of Baal! This one speaks a little Carthaginian!

I'm Hanno, I'm from Carthage.

AG. Quid ait? MI. Hannonem se esse ait Carthagine,

580 Carthaginiensis Mytthumbalis filium.

HA. Hello. MI. Salutat. HA. Don't know much Punic, do you?

MI. Doni vult tibi dare hic nescioquid. audin pollicitarier?

AG. Saluta hunc rursus Punice verbis meis.

MI. Halo, inquit hic tibi verbis suis.

585 HA. Maybe you could help me … MI. Istuc tibi sit potius quam mihi.

AG. Quid ait? MI. Miseram esse praedicat buccam sibi.

fortasse medicos nos esse arbitrarier.

AG. Si ita est, nega esse; nolo ego errare hospitem.

roga numquid opus sit. MI. Tu qui sonam non habes,

591 **my reason for…my friend's kid…:** The sounds of Hanno's halting speech are transferred into Milphio's *mures Africanos* (line 592).

593 **in pompam:** "for the parade." As their empire grew, the Romans became increasingly fond of showcasing exotic foreign animals at their games. In fact, it is quite likely that African animals like panthers and elephants would have been seen by the Romans during the triumphal games (*ludi*) for Scipio Africanus' victory over Carthage in the Second Punic War, perhaps only a few years before the production of the *Poenulus*. African mice, however, as in line 592, are clearly just Milphio's making fun of Africa's reputation for exotic beasts.

  aedilibus: *aediles* were the Roman officials in charge of organizing and paying for public games.

594 **look! can you…nuisance:** is translated in 595 as a strange list of things that Milphio says Hanno is trying to sell: *ligulas* (*ligula, -ae,* f., "spoon"), *canalis* (= *canales,* from *canalis, canalis,* f., "sewer pipe"), *nuces* "nuts." Milphio is stereotyping Phoenicians and Carthaginians as haggling hucksters, unscrupulous traders, who would sell anything for a profit. Merchants and trade, especially foreign trade (Phoenicians and Carthaginians were arguably the ancient world's most successful and famous merchants), were often looked down on by Romans because of the potential for fraud in dealing inferior or underweight goods. The Romans frequently accused the Carthaginians of being shady dealers, and even coined a phrase for the absolute lowest degree of untrustworthiness, *fides Punica.*

596 **veneant:** *veneo, venire,* "to be sold."

597 **this is hopeless! opes habet:** These lines are completely our own, including the Latin, to serve as a way to fill out Milphio's stereotype of Hanno as a wealthy merchant. Milphio says, in essence, "He's loaded!"

598 **oh crap, I suppose…Latin:** created to set up Milphio's most outrageous mistranslation in 600–601 with the words *cratim, supponas,* and *lapides.*

  sis: = *si vis,* "please."

599 **quod:** the antecedent *id,* direct object of *feceris,* has been omitted by Plautus.

600 **cratim:** *cratis, cratis,* f., "crate," "basket."

  ut iubeas: understand *orat* from the previous sentence, which introduces *ut* + subjunctive.

600–601 **se…sese:** reflexive pronouns referring to the subject of *orat,* Hanno.

602 An irate Hanno finally translates Milphio's Latin to show how ludicrously and maliciously Milphio has been misrepresenting him to Agorastocles.

606 **nequam:** an indeclinable adjective meaning "worthless."

607 **qui inrideas:** The subjunctive is required in a relative clause of characteristic; this can be translated, "you, who are the sort to mock…"

608 **te hominem…sycophantam:** accusatives of exclamation showing Milphio's sputtering rage at Hanno. *sycophanta, -ae,* m., "swindler," "impostor." From Milphio's point of view Hanno has been especially dishonest since he concealed his knowledge of Latin and allowed Milphio to say all those nasty things (for which Milphio is now in big trouble).

609 **captatum:** an accusative supine formed from the fourth principal part of *capto, captare.* Such a construction often occurs with a verb of movement and expresses purpose: "to try to entrap" (us).

  migdilix: No one knows what this means, but since Milphio is using it to describe Hanno it is surely nothing good.

590   quid in hanc venistis urbem aut quid quaeritis?

HA. My reason for … AG. Quid ait? HA. My friend's kid … AG. Quid venit?

MI. Non audis? mures Africanos praedicat

in pompam ludis dare se velle aedilibus.

HA. Look! Can you stop being such a nuisance! AG. Quid nunc ait?

595   MI. Ligulas, canalis ait se advexisse et nuces:

nunc orat operam ut des sibi, ut ea veneant.

AG. Mercator credo est. HA. This is hopeless! MI. Opes habet.

HA. Oh crap, I suppose I'll just speak to you in Latin! MI. Hem! cave sis feceris

quod hic te orat. AG. Quid ait aut quid orat? expedi.

600   MI. Sub cratim ut iubeas se supponi atque eo

lapides imponi multos, ut sese neces.

HA. I did not say that you should put me under a crate and pile rocks on me

until I die.

AG. Narra, quid est? quid ait?

MI. Non hercle nunc quidem quicquam scio.

605   HA. At ut scias, nunc dehinc Latine iam loquar.

servum hercle te esse oportet et nequam et malum,

hominem peregrinum atque advenam qui inrideas.

MI. At hercle te hominem et sycophantam et subdolum,

qui huc advenisti nos captatum, migdilix,

610 **bisulci lingua quasi proserpens bestia:** Plautus gives Milphio an artistic bit of rage, for *bisulci lingua* carries a double meaning. Milphio certainly means to say Hanno has a "forked tongue," (thus the snake reference) in the sense that he's a deceiver, or as we put it, "He speaks out of both sides of his mouth." But on another level, the "forked tongue" image works to express the Carthaginians' renown as a people fluent in many languages, a talent that Hanno himself mentions at lines 565–566. So in this sense *bisulci lingua* means Hanno is bilingual. Milphio sees this language facility as yet another sign of a deceitful Carthaginian. After this line Milphio was so uncharacteristically quiet (more than forty lines in the original) that we sent him offstage until line 643.

611 **face:** This form of the singular imperative sometimes occurs in pre-classical writers (classical singular imperative of *facere* is *fac*). *fac* + subjunctive ("be sure to…") is one way to give a command. Thus, *linguam compescas face* means "make sure that you hold your tongue!" or in more concise English, "Shut up!"

612 **meis consanguineis:** "(to speak) to my relative"; a plural translated as a singular.

613 **Carthagini:** the locative form, "in (or at) Carthage." Milphio revealed this at lines 524–526.

615 **si quid opus est:** There is an unexpressed *tibi* here. "If there is need of anything for you" or in better English, "If you need anything."

616 **popularitatis causa:** "for the sake of our common citizenship."

617–618 It is pure comic irony that the first person Hanno speaks to here should be the very one he's seeking.

618 **hem:** an exclamation of surprise and astonishment, often used when a character meets up with someone unexpectedly.

619 Agorastocles' response is in indirect discourse after *audio* from Hanno's last line.

   Antidamae: the genitive of Antidamas, the man who bought Agorastocles from a pirate and adopted him as his son. The other half of the *tessera* (explained at line 546) should have been left to Agorastocles by Antidamas.

   itast: = *ita est.*

620 **eccam attuli:** "Look, I brought [mine]."

621 **agedum:** *dum* added to the imperative *age*, thus intensifying it: "Come on!!"

   eamdem: In Plautus' original, Agorastocles tells Hanno here that he's got the other half inside his house, but that doesn't make for a very vivid recognition scene so we had Agorastocles produce the other half on the spot.

622 **multum:** an adverbial accusative here and, although it can not really be translated into English, it conveys the special warmth in Hanno's greeting: "a hearty hello."

623 **patritus:** *patritus, -a, -um,* "belonging to one's father."

624–625 Agorastocles acknowledges the ties of familial hospitality passed down from generation to generation. Among Greeks and Romans it was an obligation, not a choice.

626 **quae:** *ea,* the antecedent of *quae* (and the object of *dent*), has dropped out.

627 **qui:** This is the adverbial *qui* meaning "how."

630 We find out that Antidamas actually adopted Agorastocles.

631 Hanno asks Agorastocles about his biological parents from Carthage.

   tuum: = *tuorum.*

633 **vellem tibi:** "I would wish for your sake…" The *tibi* is a dative of interest.

636 **frater patruelis:** When *frater* or *soror* is combined with the adjective *patruelis* the phrase means "cousin."

639 **ludenti puero:** This is dative because it is in apposition to *tibi* from the previous line.

   quod: The antecedent of this relative pronoun is *signum.*

   memordit: from *mordeo, -ere.*

610 bisulci lingua quasi proserpens bestia.

      AG. Maledicta hinc aufer, linguam compescas face.

      meis consanguineis nolo te iniuste loqui.

      Carthagini ego sum gnatus, ut tu sis sciens.

      HA. O mi popularis, salve! **AG.** Et tu edepol, quisquis es.

615 et si quid opus est, quaeso, dic atque impera

      popularitatis causa. **HA.** Habeo gratiam.

      sed ecquem adulescentem tu hic novisti Agorastoclem?

      AG. Ego sum ipsus quem tu quaeris! **HA.** Hem, quid ego audio?

      AG. Antidamae gnatum me esse. **HA.** Si itast, tesseram

620 conferre si vis hospitalem, eccam attuli.

      AG. Agedum huc ostende. est par probe, nam eamdem habeo.

      HA. O mi hospes, salve multum! nam mihi tuus pater

      patritus ergo hospes Antidamas fuit.

      AG. Ergo hic apud me hospitium tibi praebebitur.

625 nam hau repudio hospitium neque Carthaginem,

      unde sum oriundus. **HA.** Di dent tibi omnes quae velis.

      quid ais? qui potuit fieri ut Carthagini

      gnatus sis?

      AG. Surruptus sum illinc. hic me Antidamas hospes tuus

630 emit et is me sibi adoptavit filium.

      HA. Dic mihi, ecquid meministi tuum parentum nomina?

      AG. Ampsigura mater mihi fuit, Iahon pater.

      HA. Patrem atque matrem viverent vellem tibi.

      AG. An mortui sunt? **HA.** Factum, quod ego aegre tuli.

635 nam mihi sobrina Ampsigura tua mater fuit;

      pater tuus, is erat frater patruelis meus.

      sed si ita est, ut tu sis Iahonis filius,

      signum esse oportet in manu laeva tibi,

      ludenti puero quod memordit simia.

642 **iterum mihi gnatus videor:** "I seem to myself to have been born again." It is not clear what Hanno means by this, but he is obviously happy upon finding Agorastocles.

643 At this point Milphio returns to the stage. He was left without a speaking part for so long (more than thirty lines, which is most unlike Milphio) that we sent him offstage in our production. Seeing his master and Hanno getting along wonderfully he is sarcastic here.

644 **mi[hi] in mentem:** "into the mind for me," or in better English, "to my mind."
modo: "just now."

645 **opust:** = *opus est.*
quid lubet: "what is pleasing" or in better English, "what you want." *lubet = libet*, several forms of which appear over the next few lines.

646 **quid est negoti:** "what the situation is" or "what's up."
potin: = *potesne.*
subdolus: Milphio wants to use what he sees as Hanno's natural Carthaginian craftiness as a means of catching the pimp in a trap.

647 **inimico possum:** Understand *fieri subdolus* to complete the thought of this sentence.
amicost: = *amico est.*
insipientia: "stupidity."

648 **male faxim:** *facere male* can mean "to do harm to (someone)." The someone is not expressed here but it is Agorastocles' enemy (the pimp), whom Milphio mentioned in the previous line. Translate the adjective *lubens* as an adverb: "gladly."

649 **ab lenone:** "[a girl] from the pimp ['s house]."

651 **ei:** This dative of interest refers to the pimp.

652 **hic:** Milphio refers to Agorastocles with the demonstrative pronoun *hic* since Agorastocles is standing right next to him.

653 **incestavit:** from *incesto, -are*, "to violate, to make impure (i.e., to have sex with)."

655–664 Milphio does not know that Adelphasium and Anterastilis are Hanno's daughters, so he concocts a story (that Hanno will lay claim to these two girls as his own kidnapped daughters) that is in fact true. Hanno is overcome by emotion at thinking about the sorry plight of his family. His sincere grief is interpreted by Milphio as a stunning display of acting.

655 **adlegemus:** *adlego, -are*, "to use, employ."
parvolas: = *parvulas*, "when they were very young."

657 *adserere manu* means to lay a hand upon someone to claim them, and with *liberali causa* it means "to claim someone as free."

659 **mihi:** dative of possession: "To me there are two daughters…" or in better English, "I have two daughters."

660 **una:** adverb, "at the same time."

661 **id:** the subject of *placet* referring to Hanno's "performance" in the role of father and claimant of the girls. In Milphio's eyes, Hanno is playing his part to perfection (see line 664).

662 **eu:** "fine," "splendid."
mortalem catum: exclamations or outbursts are often in the accusative case.

664 **ut:** "how." This use of *ut* does takes an indicative verb, not a subjunctive.
quo: rather than *ut*, introduces a purpose clause containing a comparative (such as *facilius* "more easily").
illud: like *id* above in line 661, refers to Milphio's plan, which is here highlighted by use of *gestu*, a "stage gesture." Gesture was one of the great skills required of an actor on the ancient comic stage, especially since masks and distance from the audience probably prevented the use of facial expressions. Elaborate movement and gesture, like what Hanno must be doing here, conveyed the emotions of the actor. Milphio makes a joke about the acting profession in a situation where an actor (Hanno) has been asked to be an actor (the father who lost his daughters) in a role that he is already playing.

640 ostende: inspiciam. di deaeque! mei fili fratris!

AG. Mi patrue, salve! **HA.** Et tu salve, Agorastocles.

iterum mihi gnatus videor, cum te repperi.

MI. Pol istam rem vobis bene evenisse gaudeo.

festivum facinus venit mi in mentem modo.

645 **HA.** Quid id est? **MI.** Tua opust opera. **HA.** Dic mihi, quid lubet:

quid est negoti? **MI.** Potin tu fieri subdolus?

HA. Inimico possum, amicost insipientia.

MI. Inimicus hercle est huius. **HA.** Male faxim lubens.

MI. Amat ab lenone hic. **HA.** Facere sapienter puto.

650 **MI.** Leno hic habitat vicinus. **HA.** Male faxim lubens.

MI. Ei duae puellae sunt meretrices servolae

sorores: earum hic alteram efflictim perit

neque eam incestavit umquam. **HA.** Acerba amatiost.

MI. Nunc hoc consilium capio et hanc fabricam paro,

655 ut te adlegemus, filias dicas tuas

surruptasque esse parvolas Carthagine,

manu liberali causa ambas adseras

quasi filiae tuae sint ambae. intellegis?

HA. Intellego hercle. nam mihi item gnatae duae

660 cum nutrice una sunt surruptae parvolae.

MI. Lepide hercle adsimulas! iam in principio id mihi placet.

HA. Pol magis quam vellem. **MI.** Eu hercle mortalem catum,

malum crudumque et callidum et subdolum!

ut adflet, quo illud gestu faciat facilius!

666 **statura…:** the first of several ablatives of description in lines 666–667.

aquilost: = *aquilo est. aquilus, -a, -um,* "dark," "swarthy." We are not sure if Giddenis is being described as having skin coloring noticeably darker than other Carthaginians or if this description is of a typical Carthaginian, and thus a joke playing on the qualities by which one might recognize any Carthaginian. See director's notes for our theatrical interpretation.

669 **vin:** = *visne.*

672–673 **nuntiate ut prodeat foras Giddeneni:** The subject of *prodeat* is Giddenis and the dative *Giddeneni* is the indirect object of the verb *nuntiate.*

5.3

674 **te proximust:** = *te proximus est; te* is accusative. Milphio is "closest" to Giddenis not only in housing (they live next door to each other) but in social rank (they're both slaves).

675 **novistin…illunc:** = *novistine…illum.* Literally, "Do you know that man, who he is?" We would say "Do you know who that man is?"

tunicatum: See note on *tunicis* at line 557.

676 **pro:** here not a preposition but an exclamation: "Oh!"

678 **ecce autem mala:** "Look at that, she's a cunning one!" *malus* occasionally means "bad" in the sense of "mischievous" or "sly."

679 **praestrigiator:** *praestrigiator, praestrigiatoris,* m., "trickster," "conjurer."

680 **omnis:** = *omnes,* accusative plural. Milphio is amazed that everyone turns out to know Hanno, as if he had somehow charmed them all with a spell.

681 **insperatissume:** = *insperatissime,* the vocative of the superlative of *insperatus,* "unhoped for," "unlooked for," "unexpected."

683 **contemplarier:** = *contemplari.*

684 **cognoscin:** = *cognoscisne.*

685 **novi:** *nosco, -ere, novi, notum* means "to get to know," "to find out" in the present tense; in the perfect tense it means "to have found out," "to have gotten to know," and so it should be translated as "to know," "to recognize."

687 **Aphrodisia:** is plural and so cannot be the subject of the sentence. Translate it in apposition with *festus dies.*

688 **impetrarunt:** = *impetraverunt,* "they've succeeded in their request" (to make Venus favorable to them); i.e., the goddess has given them their father.

hic hic: The first means "here," the second "he."

689 **eho an huius:** *eho* is an exclamation of surprise, and a question introduced by *an* also shows an element of surprise or excitement. Agorastocles is a little slow at figuring out the connection between Hanno and the two sisters. *huius* refers to Hanno.

ut praedicas: *praedico, -are,* "to make known," "to declare"; *ut,* "as."

665 HA. Sed earum nutrix, qua sit facie, mi expedi.

MI. Statura hau magna, corpore aquilost. HA. Ipsa east.

MI. Specie venusta, ore atque oculis pernigris.

HA. Formam quidem hercle verbis depinxti probe.

MI. Vin eam videre? HA. Filias malo meas.

670 sed i atque evoca illam; si eae meae sunt filiae,

si illarum est nutrix, me continuo noverit.

MI. Heus, ecquis hic est? nuntiate ut prodeat

foras Giddeneni. est qui illam conventam esse vult.

5.3 [original lines 1120–1173, with cuts]

The girls' nurse, Giddenis, recognizes Hanno, her old master, and there is a joyful reunion, although he is a little concerned that his daughters are at the temple of Venus celebrating Aphrodite Day. Agorastocles gets Hanno to promise Adelphasium's hand in marriage.

GIDDENIS. Quis pultat? MI. Qui te proximust. GI. Quid vis? MI. Eho,

675 novistin tu illunc tunicatum hominem qui sit?

GI. Nam quem ego aspicio? pro supreme Iuppiter!

erus meus hic quidem est, mearum alumnarum pater,

Hanno Carthaginiensis. MI. Ecce autem mala!

praestrigiator hic quidem Poenus probust,

680 perduxit omnis ad suam sententiam.

GI. O mi ere, salve, Hanno, insperatissume

mihi tuisque filiis, salve atque … eho,

mirari noli neque me contemplarier.

cognoscin Giddenenem ancillam tuam?

685 HA. Novi. sed ubi sunt meae gnatae? id scire expeto.

GI. Apud aedem Veneris. HA. Quid ibi faciunt? dic mihi.

GI. Aphrodisia hodie Veneris est festus dies.

MI. Pol satis scio, impetrarunt, quando hic hic adest.

AG. Eho an huius sunt illae filiae? GI. Ita ut praedicas.

690 **tua pietas:** Giddenis, having answered Agorastocles' question, speaks to Hanno again.

691 **cum huc:** *huc*, "to this place." Plautus does not always use the subjunctive in a *cum*-clause.

in ipso tempore: we would say "in the nick of time."

692 **mutarentur nomina:** shows (along with *facerent* in the next line) that this is one half of a present contrary-to-fact condition, whose other half is omitted. Giddenis tells Hanno, "[If you hadn't shown up,] their names would be being changed…"

693 **genere…corpore:** *genere* is ablative after *indignum*; *corpore* is ablative of means with *quaestus, -us, m.*, "profit," "income," "living." If Hanno had not arrived the two sisters would have become official prostitutes that very day at the Aphrodisia.

694 **mommy!:** One of Hanno's slaves turns out to be Giddenis' long-lost son. They embrace, but Agorastocles can't understand the English/Punic they speak to one another. (For original Punic lines, see Appendix.)

697–698 Hanno now orders Milphio to take Hanno's slaves with him into the house of Agorastocles, who explains that he wants dinner prepared.

698–700 Agorastocles is annoyed at Milphio's sluggishness in responding to his orders. *facias* and *memores* are both dependent on *mavelim* (= *malim*): "I'd rather you…"

701 **go:** Milphio does know at least one more word of Hanno's language. See Appendix for original "Punic" text.

detrudam ad molas: "I'll shove you down into the mills," one of the least desirable work environments for slaves. Milphio is anxious to boss slaves around and to make their lives miserable, like his has been. Interestingly enough this is the last we will see of Milphio in our version of this play, but even in Plautus' original Milphio only returns briefly at the end of this scene for a couple of snide comments, after which he departs for good. While that might seem odd for the purposes of the plot, there is probably a very simple reason. In Plautus' day, a limited number of actors performed multiple parts in the same play. A look back over this play will show that the actor who played Milphio probably played either Lycus or Antamoenides, with whom he never appears onstage, but both of whom will reenter the play soon after Milphio's exit.

702 **faxo:** = *fecero*.

703 **audin:** = *audisne*. The slaves have exited leaving Hanno and Agorastocles alone onstage. The young lover takes the opportunity to ask his uncle about a possible marriage to Adelphasium. It was common in the ancient world that marital arrangements would be negotiated by the men without much involvment or consideration of the bride-to-be. In this case Agorastocles would be marrying his first cousin, but many ancient cultures allowed such an arrangement, and families often desired it as a way of maintaining or restoring family ties. Agorastocles' request has a slightly sneaky side in the context of our play, since he knows that Adelphasium does not like him, so he asks her father who, not knowing their history of antagonism, is just happy to get the family together again.

704 **despondeas:** subjunctive can be used in polite commands: "Please betroth…"

705 **habeto:** The future imperative of *habere* always means "consider." *pactam* is from *pango, -ere, pepigi, pactum*, "to strike," as also in the English metaphor, "to strike a deal."

spondesne…spondeo: the traditional question and response of a Roman betrothal.

708 **cupio:** The present tense, especially when used with an adverb of time (like *iamdudum*), can describe an action that started in the past and continues in the present: "I've been wanting that for a long time."

709 **eccas:** a combination of *ecce* "look!" and *eas* "those women."

haecin: = *haecne*.

710 **quantae e quantillis:** Hanno is amazed at the sight of his daughters, whom he last saw when they were small children. This also represents the age-old wonderment that children grow up so "fast" to become adults.

690 tua pietas nobis plane auxilio fuit,

cum huc advenisti hodie in ipso tempore;

namque hodie earum mutarentur nomina

facerentque indignum genere quaestum corpore.

PUER. Mommy! **GI.** Baal be praised! It's my boy!

695 **AG.** Quid illi locuti sunt inter se? dic mihi.

HA. Matrem hic salutat suam, haec autem hunc filium.

Tu abduc hosce intro et una nutricem simul

iube hanc abire hinc ad te. **AG.** Fac quod imperat.

MI. Abeo igitur. **AG.** Facias modo quam memores mavelim.

700 patruo advenienti cena curetur volo.

MI. Go vos, quos ego iam detrudam ad molas,

ego faxo hospitium hoc leniter laudabitis.

AG. Audin tu, patrue? dico, ne dictum neges:

tuam mihi maiorem filiam despondeas.

705 **HA.** Pactam rem habeto. **AG.** Spondesne igitur? **HA.** Spondeo.

AG. Mi patrue, salve. nam nunc es plane meus.

nunc, patrue, si vis tuas videre filias,

me sequere. **HA.** Iamdudum equidem cupio et te sequor.

AG. Sed eccas video ipsas. **HA.** Haecin meae sunt filiae?

710 quantae e quantillis iam sunt factae!

5.4

711 **operae pretium:** "worthwhile" (literally, "the price of effort").

    amabilitati: *amabilitas*, *amabilitatis*, f., "the state of being lovable," "attractiveness."

    animum adiceret: *adicio, -ere* (= *ad* + *iacio*), "to throw (his mind) towards." We might translate "set his mind on." The verb is subjunctive because its subject (*qui,* which has *cuivis* as an antecedent) is indefinite.

712 **qui…eo visere:** pre-classical Latin does occasionally use the infinitive to show purpose. *eo,* "to there." *qui* refers to the same person as in line 711.

713 **tus, murrinus:** frankincense (*tus, turis,* n.) and myrrh (*murra, -ae,* f.; the adjective "derived from myrrh" is *murrinus, -a, -um*), burned in heaps on the altars, were essential elements in any lavish festival. Throughout these lines, Adelphasium, the more serious sister, is interested in the official rites of prostitution, the religious and spiritual elements of the profession.

714 **hau sordere:** *hau* = *haud*. The essential idea of *sordere* is "to be dirty" (the root of "sordid").

718 **certo enim:** "that's for sure, because…"

    quod: "as far as."

719 **pulchre:** can mean not only that they were "beautifully" dressed, but also that they were "thoroughly" or "splendidly" outstanding (*praepotentes*). In contrast to her sister, the fatuous Anterastilis is concerned with more superficial things about the Aphrodisia, like how much prettier they were than the other prostitutes.

720 **pacisque potentes:** Venus granted them her peace (goodwill), unlike Lycus' experience (218ff.).

721–722 **ab iuventute inibi inridiculo habitae:** "we were not considered a laughingstock by the young men there." Grammatically speaking, *inridiculo* is a predicative dative ("for a joke"), but it can be translated as if it were nominative.

724 Adelphasium has had enough of rejoicing, and now she reverts to her usual moralizing.

    uti: = *ut.*

725 Easier word order would be *et pol ego* ("and I do too"), *cum gnosco* (= *nosco*) *quibus ingeniis [nos] atque aliae sumus. ingeniis* is an ablative of characteristic or description. Although *nosco* is the main verb of a *cum*-clause and *sumus* is the main verb of an indirect statement, neither one is subjunctive. This is common in Plautus.

    Adelphasium is overly proud of her freeborn status, which doesn't seem to have done her much good up to now, but does explain her "holier-than-thou," snobbish attitude that she put on in Act 1.2, especially at lines 101–104.

726 **eo…genere, ut:** *genere* is an ablative of description. Adjectival uses of *is, ea, id* may often be translated as "such"; *ut* introduces a result clause.

727–729 Hanno, unnoticed by the sisters, begins another prayer to the gods. After a while, Agorastocles cuts him off.

727 **alisque:** *alo, -ere,* "to sustain," "to support," "to cherish."

728 **da:** translate as "make."

    agundis: = *agendis.*

729 **quibus…carui:** the fact that *careo, -ere, carui* takes the ablative explains the case of *quibus* (which refers to Adelphasium and Anterastilis).

730 **faxo:** = *fecero.* Translate as "I'll make sure."

731 **obnoxius:** does not mean "obnoxious," it means "liable to," "at the mercy of."

733 **ne lacruma:** = *ne lacrima.* Hanno cries at the mere thought of his daughters.

734 **ut volup est:** *ut,* "how"; *volup* may be translated as "pleasurable."

    cluet: *clueo, -ere* means "to be known as," "to be called."

5.4 [original lines 1174–1279, with cuts]

Adelphasium and Anterastilis return from the temple of Venus where the priest prophesied that they would soon be freed. Hanno marvels at the women his daughters have become, but he keeps his true identity concealed until the end of the scene. Meanwhile Agorastocles continues to woo Adelphasium, with little success.

ADE. Fuit hodie operae pretium cuivis qui amabilitati animum adiceret

oculis epulas dare, delubrum qui hodie ornatum eo visere venit.

aras tus, murrinus, omnis odor

complebat. hau sordere visust

715 festus dies, Venus, nec tuum fanum:

tantus ibi clientarum erat numerus,

quae ad Calydoniam venerant Venerem.

ANTE. Certo enim, quod quidem ad nos duas

attinuit, praepotentes pulchre

720 pacisque potentes, soror, fuimus,

neque ab iuventute inibi inridiculo

habitae, quod pol,

soror, ceteris omnibus factumst.

ADE. Malim istuc aliis videatur, quam uti tu te, soror, conlaudes.

725 ANTE. Spero equidem. ADE. Et pol ego, cum, ingeniis quibus sumus atque

aliae, gnosco;

eo sumus gnatae genere, ut deceat nos esse a culpa castas.

HA. Iuppiter, qui genus colis alisque hominum, per quem vivimus,

da diem hunc sospitem, quaeso, rebus meis agundis,

ut quibus annos multos carui quasque e patria …

730 AG. Omnia faciet Iuppiter faxo,

nam mi est obnoxius et me

metuit. HA. Tace quaeso.

AG. Ne lacruma, patrue.

ANTE. Vt volup est homini, mea soror, si quod agit cluet victoria;

735 **praestitimus:** *praesto, -are, praestiti, praestitum* can mean "to offer," "to show," but usually only in the presence of an accusative object. Here, it has its other meaning, "to excel," "to outshine."

736 **eo:** "to such an extent," "so." *videre* is not an infinitive but the alternative form of *videris*, the second-person singular, present tense, indicative mood, passive voice.

737 Agorastocles is once again overjoyed to hear anything that Adelphasium says.

patruissime: a superlative (in the vocative) found nowhere else: "my uncliest uncle!" Of course, "uncle" and *patruus* are nouns, not adjectives, and so they would not usually have a superlative form.

738 **ut sapit:** "how smart she is!"

739 Hanno takes Agorastocles' comment as confirmation that the sisters are in fact his daughters since they are so smart. Inherent in the term *ingenium* is the ancient belief that a person's nature, intelligence, and personality were the product of natural family ties, just as one's appearance is obviously hereditary. But notice that while Hanno is claiming that Adelphasium is showing "she's a chip off the old block," Agorastocles claims that he is now the source of her wisdom and that she forgot all she ever learned from Hanno back in her childhood.

740 **abusast:** = *abusa est*, from *abutor, abuti, abusus sum*, "to misuse," "to abuse," "to use up." This verb usually takes an ablative (as *utor* does), but here it takes an accusative.

741 **hinc:** "from here," that is, from Agorastocles himself and his own passion for her.

742 **nimiae voluptatist:** = *voluptati est. nimius, -a, -um,* "excessive," "too much."

portentumst: = *portentum est*, from *portendo, -ere,* "to predict."

744 **nos fore:** Agorastocles' quip in the previous line doesn't break the grammar of Anterastilis' speech. In this line we hear, in indirect speech, what the fortune-teller said to them. *fore* is a frequent substitute for longer forms of the future infinitive of *esse*; in this case, it would be *futuras esse*.

invito domino nostro: an ablative absolute.

745 A more easily understood word order would be *hau scio qui sperem id, nisi di aut parentes faxint quid*. Note the irony of Anterastilis suggesting that after all these years only the gods or their parents could save them now, when her father is just across the stage. This plays with the audience's awareness of the facts and their anticipation of the recognition scene (father and daughter reunion) that is about to occur.

faxint: = *fecerint*, future perfect.

qui: an old alternative for *quo modo*, "how."

746 **mea fiducia:** ablative, "in his (the soothsayer's) reliance on me."

747 **sequere hac:** As in Act 1.2, the women begin to leave but are stopped by the men. Only now do the sisters notice the presence of Hanno and Agorastocles.

748 **nisi piget:** "if it's not unpleasant," "if you don't mind."

749 **quis revocat:** Adelphasium of course does not recognize Hanno, and Agorastocles is not about to give away the secret.

occasiost: = *occasio est. occasio, occasionis*, f., "opportunity": "He's got his chance…"

750 **homost:** = *homo est.*

752 **bonus bonis bene feceris:** another of Adelphasium's morals: "you, a good man, will act well towards good people." In Plautus, the future perfect (*feceris*) often has the force of a simple future.

753 **ut:** translate it as "how" with *ducam* in the next line: "…how I would marry…"

754 **foras:** "outdoors" when motion from inside is involved (as in line 548). When one is already outside, the word is *foris* as in line 867.

735 sicut nos hodie inter alias praestitimus pulchritudine.

ADE. Stulta, soror, magis es quam volo. Tune eo pulchra videre, obsecro?

AG. Patrue mi patruissime!

HA. Quid est? AG. Est lepida et lauta. ut sapit!

HA. Ingenium patris habet quod sapit.

740 AG. Quae res? iam diu edepol sapientiam tuam haec quidem abusast.

nunc hinc sapit, hinc sentit quidquid sapit, ex meo amore.

ANTE. Nimiae voluptatist quod in extis nostris portentumst, soror,

quodque haruspex de ambabus dixit … AG. Velim de me aliquid dixerit!

ANTE. Nos fore invito domino nostro diebus paucis liberas.

745 id ego, nisi quid di aut parentes faxint, qui sperem hau scio.

AG. Mea fiducia hercle haruspex, patrue, his promisit, scio,

libertatem, quia me amare hanc scit. ADE. Soror, sequere hac. ANTE. Sequor.

HA. Prius quam abitis, vos volo ambas. nisi piget, consistite.

ADE. Quis revocat? AG. Qui bene vult vobis facere. ADE. Facere occasiost.

750 sed quis homost? AG. Amicus vobis. ADE. Qui quidem inimicus non sit.

AG. Bonus est hic homo, mea voluptas. ADE. Pol istum malim quam malum.

AG. Multa bona vult vobis facere. ADE. Bonus bonis bene feceris.

AG. Patrue mi, ita me di amabunt, ut ego, si sim Iuppiter,

iam hercle ego illam uxorem ducam et Iunonem extrudam foras.

755 **pudice...cogitate...commode:** "modestly...well thought out...aptly."

756 **meast:** = *mea est.* Hanno repeats his conviction (from line 739) that Adelphasium's speaking ability shows that she's his daughter.

757 Hanno, eager to get on with the plot, asks Agorastocles if he should "test" his daughters by pretending to haul them off to court. Agorastocles agrees, but tells him to make it short, since the audience (*qui sedent*) is thirsty (*sitiunt*). Plautus wants to draw out the fun a little longer and get in one more good trick where the characters are confused and the audience enjoys a superiority of knowledge.

758 **quid istic? quod faciundumst cur non agimus?:** "Very well then! Why aren't we doing what must be done?" After this (spoken to Agorastocles), Hanno confronts the sisters.

759 Agorastocles first threatens Adelphasium, but after a pause he changes to his usual tone.

760 Agorastocles seems to be confused. Perhaps he wanted to launch into an extended speech, as he did at the ends of Act 1.2 and Act 3.2.

761 **nisi honestiust prehendi:** *honestiust* = *honestius est.* "Unless it's more decent to be hauled off to jail."

762 **illi:** = *illic,* "there," "in that place," i.e., in the courtroom.

763 **etiam:** shows indignation. Adelphasium is annoyed that Agorastocles, of whom she has a very low opinion, is joining in the lawsuit.

   latrant: *latro, -are,* "to bark" at something or someone (in the accusative).

   at tu hercle adludiato: "Come on, then, play the game!" Agorastocles takes Adelphasium's metaphor farther. *adludiato* is a future imperative of *adludio, -are,* "to play."

764 **dato...obicito:** both of these are future imperatives.

   pro: "instead of," "in the place of."

   offa: *offa, -ae,* f., "morsel of food."

   osse: *os, ossis,* n., "bone."

766 **fures:** *fur, furis,* m., "thief." Hanno accuses the sisters of hiding his daughters (themselves, that is) from him. The sisters of course will admit to no such wrongdoing, but it offers a nice little legal joke of the sort Plautus loves. Under skewed logic, they did in fact steal Hanno's daughters by staying separated from him, though against their will.

767 **celavistis clam me:** *celo, -are,* "to hide," uses two accusatives: one for what is hidden (*filias meas*), one for the person from whom it is hidden (*me*). *clam,* "in secret."

768 All the accusatives in this line still modify *filias* from the line above.

   summoque genere gnatas: "born in the highest class of society."

769 **penes nos:** "in us," "in our characters."

770 Agorastocles asks for a kiss as a guarantee (*pignus, -oris,* n.) that she isn't lying.

771 **nil tecum ago:** "I'm not dealing at all with you." Adelphasium is still angry that Agorastocles is part of this lawsuit. He tries to tell her how important he is to the case.

772 **pro hoc:** "on his behalf."

774 **servas:** in apposition to *filias;* translate it as "as slaves."

776 **satis iam sunt maceratae:** "They've been sufficiently tenderized." Agorastocles nudges Hanno and agrees that they should reveal the truth.

777 **misera timeo:** Adelphasium is sarcastic: "I'm *so* scared."

778–779 Hanno tells his daughters the truth only after two lines of pious prayer to the gods.

778 **boni:** a partitive genitive after *quod:* "what (of) good the gods give me."

   danunt: = *dant.*

779 **est aequum:** "it is right," introducing an indirect statement whose subject is *nos.*

755 ut pudice verba fecit, cogitate et commode,

ut modeste orationem praebuit! **HA.** Certo haec meast.

Pergo etiam temptare? **AG.** In pauca confer: sitiunt qui sedent.

HA. Quid istic? quod faciundumst cur non agimus? in ius vos voco.

AG. Nunc pol ego te ulciscar probe, nam faxo … mea eris sponsa.

760 sed illud quidem volui dicere … immo hercle dixi quod volebam.

HA. Moramini. in ius vos voco, nisi honestiust prehendi.

ADE. Quid in ius vocas nos? **ANTE.** Quid tibi debemus? **AG.** Dicet illi.

ADE. Etiam me meae latrant canes? **AG.** At tu hercle adludiato:

dato mihi pro offa savium, pro osse linguam obicito.

765 ita hanc canem faciam tibi oleo tranquilliorem.

HA. Ite si itis. **ANTE.** Quid nos fecimus tibi? **HA.** Fures estis ambae.

quia annos multos filias meas celavistis clam me

atque equidem ingenuas liberas summoque genere gnatas.

ADE. Numquam mecastor reperies tu istuc probrum penes nos.

770 **AG.** Da pignus, ni nunc peiieres, in savium, uter utri det.

ADE. Nil tecum ago, apscede opsecro. **AG.** Atque hercle mecum agendum est.

nam hic patruus meus est, pro hoc mihi patronus sim necesse est;

et praedicabo quomodo vos furta faciatis multa

quoque modo huius filias apud vos habeatis servas,

775 quas vos ex patria liberas surruptas esse scitis.

ADE. Vbi sunt eae? **ANTE.** Aut quas, opsecro … **AG.** Satis iam sunt maceratae.

HA. Quid si eloquamur? **AG.** Censeo hercle, patrue. **ADE.** Misera timeo.

HA. Nunc quod boni mihi di danunt, vobis vostraeque matri,

eas dis est aequum gratias nos agere sempiternas:

780 **cognatus:** "a relative," one who is "born with" the rest of the family.

781 **huiusce:** literally, "of this man here." Hanno is referring to himself.

782 **num:** at the beginning of a question, usually expecting the answer "no." Adelphasium hopes that they've stopped playing games with her and Anterastilis.
oblectant: *oblecto, -are* "to delight," "to entertain."

782–783 **at ita me di servent, ut hic pater est vester:** literally, "but so may the gods save me as he is your father." We might say, "Sure as the gods love me, he's your father!"

783 **date manus:** Agorastocles tells father and daughter to join hands.
insperate: *insperatus, -a, -um,* "unlooked for," "unexpected," is a popular adjective in recognition scenes. *insperate* is vocative, as are *cupite* and *exspectate* in line 784.

784–785 No one onstage listens to Agorastocles' complaint.

787 **sedo:** *sedo, -are,* "to settle," "to soothe," "to allay."

788 **videmur:** The passive of "to see" in Latin often means "to seem."

789 **qui:** = "how." Agorastocles tries to pry Adelphasium off Hanno's neck and onto his own.

790 **enicari:** *enico, -are (e- + neco),* "to kill." Agorastocles wants Hanno to betroth Adelphasium to him before she chokes her father to death. She at last lets go.

792 **alter alterum:** "one another," "each other."
nervum bracchialem: *nervus, -i,* m., is a knot of any kind; *bracchialis, -e* means "pertaining to or composed of arms (*bracchia*)."

793–795 Agorastocles laments the fact that all the famous painters died before they could make a portrait of this happy group. Plautus originally called on the ancient Greek muralists Apelles and Zeuxis to paint the scene, but we updated the names in order to stage more modern and recognizable art works for the audience. (See the director's notes for an explanation of our adaptation.)

794 **numero:** an adverb meaning "too soon," "untimely."
ut pingeretis: Although this expresses what they could *not* do, the English translation can also omit the negative: "…die too soon to make a painting from this tableau."

796 Hanno launches into yet another prayer to the gods, which is cut mercifully short by the blustery entrance of the enraged soldier Antamoenides.

5.5

797 **minam:** Antamoenides is justifiably mad, since he has gotten neither food nor sex in return for the *mina* of silver that he had given to the pimp (see line 232).
ultus fuero: a future perfect (we would expect *ultus ero*) of *ulciscor, -i,* "to avenge."

798 **habento scurrae ludificatui:** The soldier has his reputation to uphold. If he can't get his money back, he'll be a laughingstock. The future imperative of *habeo* has the force "consider." *scurra, -ae,* m., is a "man-about-town," a "wit," a "fashionable fellow." *ludificatui* is a predicative dative (from *ludificatus, -us,* m., "teasing").

799 **ignavissimus:** "extremely lazy."

780 vos meae estis ambae filiae et hic est cognatus vester,

huiusce fratris filius, Agorastocles. **ADE.** Amabo,

num hi falso oblectant gaudio nos? **AG.** At ita me di servent,

ut hic pater est vester. date manus. **ADE.** Salve, insperate nobis

pater, te complecti nos sine! **ANTE.** Cupite atque exspectate

785 pater, salve! **HA.** Ambae filiae sunt. **ANTE.** Amplectamur ambae.

AG. Quis me amplectetur postea? **HA.** Nunc ego sum fortunatus,

multorum annorum miserias nunc hac voluptate sedo!

ADE. Vix hoc videmur credere.

AG. Quaeso, qui lubet tam diu tenere collum?

790 omitte saltem tu altera. nolo ego istuc enicari prius quam tibi desponderit.

ADE. Mitto. **ANTE.** Sperate, salve.

HA. Condamus alter alterum ergo in nervum bracchialem.

AG. O pictores,

cur numero estis mortui, hoc exemplo ut pingeretis?

795 O Michelangelo! O Botticelli! O Rockwell!

HA. Di deaeque omnes, vobis habeo merito magnas gratias …

5.5 [original lines 1280–1337, with cuts]

Antamoenides comes storming out of Lycus' house, angry that he hasn't gotten his promised woman. Then when he sees Anterastilis, the girl he wants, wrapped around Hanno's arm, he gets the wrong idea and insults Hanno. Agorastocles, initially afraid, eventually steps in and calls out a goon to threaten Antamoenides. The soldier does not back down until set upon by Anterastilis. Suddenly all attention turns to the arrival of Lycus, whom everyone wants to abuse.

ANTAMOENIDES. Si ego minam non ultus fuero probe quam lenoni dedi,

tum profecto me sibi habento scurrae ludificatui.

is etiam me ad prandium ad se abduxit ignavissimus,

800 pro atriensi: "in the role of butler." Antamoenides ought to have been treated as a paying guest in Lycus' house, but instead was left alone like a slave.

801 edim: an alternative form for *edam*, the present subjunctive of *edo, -ere*, "to eat."

802 prandi: the short form of the genitive (*prandii*).

foras: "outside"; see the note at line 754.

803 sic dedero: "this is what I'll do."

aere militari tetigero lenunculum: literally, "I will have touched that little pimp with military bronze." It sounds as if the soldier will use his sword against the pimp. But *tango, tangere, tetigi, tactum* can also mean "to hoodwink," "to swindle," and *aes militare* refers to "military pay," so this phrase means "I'll swindle that little pimp out of my army money."

804 sed mea amica: Like most of Plautus' male characters, Antamoenides is interested in money, food, and sex. Having discussed the first two, he moves on to the third. The soldier would like to find Anterastilis, whom he requested from Lycus at line 259. But not until line 813 does he realize that she and the others are onstage.

obviam: an adverb, "in the way of," "so as to meet." It takes a dative (*mihi irato*).

805 uti sit merulea: "so that she's black and blue." *meruleus* actually means "colored like a blackbird (*merula, -ae,* f.)"; hence Anterastilis' joke in line 808.

806 atritate: "blackness." *atrior* is the comparative form of *ater, atra, atrum*, "black."

807 Aegyptini: "Ethiopian slaves."

808 sis: = *si vis*, "if you are willing," "please."

arte: "tightly."

milvos: *milvus, -i*, m., "a bird of prey." Anterastilis' comments about fearing "birds of prey" and being Hanno's "little chicken" (line 809) are references back to Antamoenides' bird simile with *merulea* at line 805.

809 ne forte: "let him not by chance," "I hope he doesn't happen to…"

me…pullum tuum: *pullus, -i*, m., "young chicken." It is in apposition to *me*.

810 ego me moror: "I'm delaying myself," "I'm wasting my time" (by ranting and raving to himself). At this point he catches sight of the whole family. He recognizes Anterastilis, but wonders who in the world Hanno can be.

812 puer cauponius: "a tavern boy." Antamoenides sees Hanno's foreign costume and can only compare him to a long-tunicked waiter. See Milphio's similar tunic references at 557 and 675.

813 satin: = *satisne.*

814 sensi nihili pendier: literally, "I have realized that I have been valued at nothing for a long time now." *pendier* is an archaic form of the present passive infinitive of *pendo, -ere*, "to weigh" or "to value"; the price at which something is valued is put in the genitive (*nihili*, the genitive of *nihilum*). Antamoenides assumes that Anterastilis, who is now clinging to another man, must never have had any thought for him.

815 baiolum: *baiolus, -i*, m., "a porter," "a servant who carries loads." Again Antamoenides calls Hanno a lowly slave. But since *puellam* and *baiolum* are both accusative, it is impossible to tell which is the subject of *amplexari* and which is the object. No matter which goes where, the arrangement is artful for the two huggers are on either side of the verb "to hug."

816 excruciandum…carnufici: a future passive participle of *excrucio, -are*, "to torture." *carnufex, carnufici*, m., "executioner" or "torturer."

817 hanc amatricem Africam: *amatrix, amatricis*, f., is usually a female lover, and so Antamoenides is insulting Hanno's clothing by calling him an "African lovergirl." He openly calls Hanno a woman (*mulier*) in the next line.

818 ecquid te pudet: *ecquid*, "is there anything that…" rather assumes that the answer is no: "Have you no shame?"

819 negotist: = *negoti est. negoti*, the shortened form of *negotii*, is a partitive genitive after *quid.*

800   ipse abiit foras, me reliquit pro atriensi in aedibus.

     ubi nec leno neque illae redeunt nec quod edim quicquam datur,

     pro maiore parte prandi pignus cepi, abii foras;

     sic dedero: aere militari tetigero lenunculum.

     sed mea amica nunc mihi irato obviam veniat velim:

805   iam pol ego illam pugnis totam faciam uti sit merulea,

     ita replebo atritate, atrior multo ut sit

     quam Aegyptini, qui cortinam ludis per circum ferunt.

     ANTE. Tene sis me arte, mea voluptas; male ego metuo milvos.

     mala illa bestiast, ne forte me auferat pullum tuum.

810   **ADE.** Vt nequeo te satis complecti, mi pater. **ANTA.** Ego me moror.

     sed quid hoc est? quid est? quid hoc est? quid ego video? quo modo?

     quis hic homo est cum tunicis longis quasi puer cauponius?

     satin ego oculis cerno? estne illa mea amica Anterastilis?

     et ea est certo. iam pridem ego me sensi nihili pendier.

815   non pudet puellam amplexari baiolum in media via?

     iam hercle ego illum excruciandum totum carnufici dabo.

     sed adire certum est hanc amatricem Africam.

     heus tu, tibi dico, mulier, ecquid te pudet?

     quid tibi negotist autem cum istac? dic mihi.

820 Hanno returns a slight insult at Antamoenides by calling him *adulescens*, which in Roman terminology is literally "a boy under military age" or "a teenager," so he is insulting the soldier's maturity.

821 Literally, "Why is there for you a touching (of) this woman with a finger?" That is, "Why are you touching her?" Antamoenides' jealous question is met with Hanno's sincere and direct answer, "Because I like to."

822–827 Antamoenides is overcome with rage and hurls a string of epithets at Hanno, not all of which can be understood; our translation is necessarily inexact. A *ligula* can be a spoon (as at line 595), the tongue of a shoe, or a type of sword. How it works as an insult is uncertain.

823 **hallex:** "big toe," or perhaps "residue of *garum* (a fish-sauce)."

824 **contrectare:** the same verb ("to caress," "to grope") that the pimp used in trying to entice Collybisca (line 387).

   mares homines: "male humans," "*real* men." *mares* is from the adjective *mas, maris,* "masculine."

825–826 literally: "Flayed sardine, of sowings, sheepskin coat, crushed olive!" No one quite knows what *sarrapis* means, unless it has something to do with the similar Greek word for a white Persian robe with purple stripes; *halagora* ("salt-market" in Greek) is likewise unclear; how the term "sheepskin coat" (*manstruca*) came to be used as a pejorative is entirely unknown, but it probably has to do with the smell, as surely do the fish and garlic references, and perhaps also the smoothness of sheepskin, which being soft and hairless could be an allusion to Hanno as effeminate.

827 **ali:** *alium, al(i)i,* n., "garlic." Although garlic was a common part of many Mediterranean diets, this rare insult from a Greek soldier against the Romans in a Roman comedy may carry with it the idea that lower class Romans ate larger than normal quantities of the important, but smelly bulb. The insult would then carry the impact of modern-day stereotypes like calling the French "frogs" because of their culture's passions for that food. On the other hand, Plautus may just like the funny references to smelly breath and the alliterative sound of *Romani remiges*.

   ulpici: *ulpicum, -i,* n. According to Pliny the Elder, an ancient naturalist, this was a Punic variety of garlic, and so at least Antamoenides' insult is culturally relevant.

828 **adulescens:** see line 820.

   malae: not "bad women" but "cheeks" (there's a difference in the length of the first vowel). Agorastocles is asking Antamoenides if his mouth itches, since he's been "scratching" it by talking so much. Lycus had a similar joke at lines 436–437.

829 **malam rem:** "trouble."

830 **quin adhibuisti:** "why didn't you use..." Antamoenides is just as angry at Agorastocles, and considers him just as much a wimp as Hanno, or more.

   dum istaec loquere: Remember that in *dum*-clauses, Latin uses the present tense (*loquere*) where English might use the past ("you spoke").

   tympanum: a small drum of some sort; the word has effeminate connotations as seen in its connection with *cinaedum* in the next line.

831 **cinaedum:** *cinaedus, i,* m., "fag," transliterated from the Greek *kinaidos,* is a standard word for a passive homosexual, usually the younger, often more effeminate, member of a homosexual couple. We use the insulting term "fag" here because the Latin word is frequently used in a derogatory sense. There is some evidence that a *kinaidos* was also a particularly effeminate type of public dancer. This could explain the reference to a *tympanum* in the last line, making the accusation of effeminacy even stronger. Homosexuality was not universally condemned by any means in Rome or Greece, but the soldier Antamoenides is oppressively heterosexual and tries to insult the masculinity of any man he finds in the company of his "girl," Anterastilis.

832 **scin:** = *scisne.*

   quam: "how," i.e., "how much of a."

   i istinc: "come out here!" Agorastocles has the power of his well-armed slave to oppose Antamoenides' physical threats. In Plautus' text Agorastocles calls for multiple slaves.

833 **fustis:** is the alternative accusative plural form of *fustes. fustis, -is,* m., "club."

   per iocum: "in jest," "as a joke."

834 **nolito:** future imperative, equivalent to *noli*. Antamoenides, saying that he was only joking, excuses himself with the same tactic that Agorastocles used at line 290. This deflation of the blustery *miles*, who then wimpishly begs forgiveness, is fairly standard in Plautus.

820 HA. Adulescens, salve. ANTA. Nolo, nihil ad te attinet.

quid tibi hanc digito tactio est? HA. Quia mihi lubet.

ANTA. Lubet? HA. Ita dico. ANTA. Ligula, i in malam crucem!

tune hic amator audes esse, hallex viri,

aut contrectare quod mares homines amant?

825 deglupta maena, sarrapis sementium,

manstruca, halagora, sampsa, tum autem plenior

ali ulpicique quam Romani remiges!

AG. Num tibi, adulescens, malae aut dentes pruriunt,

qui huic es molestus, an malam rem quaeritas?

830 ANTA. Quin adhibuisti, dum istaec loquere, tympanum?

nam te cinaedum esse arbitror magis quam virum.

AG. Scin quam cinaedus sum? i istinc, serve, foras,

ecfer fustis. ANTA. Heus tu, si quid per iocum

dixi, nolito in serium convertere.

835–838 Anterastilis cusses out Antamoenides for speaking so rudely to her father and cousin.

835 **qui:** = *quo modo.*

lubidost: = *lubido est.*

840 **magni mali:** partitive genitive after *quid* (which stands for *aliquid* after *si*).

841 Again, Plautus uses an indicative verb (*optigit*, from *optingo, -ere*) in a *cum*-clause.

e: "out of," "as a result of."

842 **bonum virum:** Agorastocles notices Lycus returning home and refers to him sarcastically.

eccum: = *ecce + eum*: "there he is!"

844 **iniuriarum:** Hanno is making a lame joke on the resemblance of sound between Agorastocles' *in ius* ("into court") and *iniuriarum*. His line literally translates as "It'd be much better (for him) to be hauled into court on the charge of wrongdoing." Where English uses a potential ("It *would* be better"), Latin in this case uses an indicative (*satius est*).

5.6 & 5.7

Note: The Latin text has two separate endings, which may have been written at different times in the play's performance history. Such a rewriting often occurs when the play is poorly received by an audience, like Aristophanes' Clouds and Terence's The Mother-in-Law. We used a combination of both endings to make our Poenulus as confrontational as possible for the live audience.

845 Lycus talks to himself (and to the audience), picking up right where he left off at lines 465–466 by reviewing how all his friends told him to hang himself to avoid being in debt to Agorastocles.

847 **idem unum convenit:** "one and the same (idea) suited…"

848 **addicar:** *addico, -ere* "to adjudge," "to assign," "to hand over." Lycus contemplates suicide rather than becoming Agorastocles' slave, and only after this line does he notice that he is not alone onstage.

851 **aio:** "I declare," introducing an indirect statement.

853 **parvolae:** = *parvulae*, "when they were very young."

854–855 Lycus pretends that he knew of the sisters' status all along, but no one believes him. *miratus fui* is an alternative form for *miratus sum* (from *miror, -ari*), introducing an indirect statement.

855 **adsereret manu:** to "grasp" someone "by the hand" was to claim that person legally as a child (or slave, or free person). See the note on lines 527–528.

856 **duplum…mihi opus est:** *opus est* is an idiom for "there is need"; the person who has the need appears in the dative (*mihi*), and the thing needed appears variously in the ablative (*suppliciis multis* in line 857), the genitive, or (as here) the nominative (*duplum*).

sume hinc quid lubet: "Take what you like from here." Lycus points to his neck (*collum, -i*, n.), as is revealed by Lycus' opening statement in this scene about hanging himself and Antamoenides' specific mention of taking payment out of Lycus' neck at line 868.

858 **rem solvam:** *solvo, -ere*, "to loosen," "to release," "to undo." In financial matters it means "to pay," and we still speak of people not in debt as *solvent* (i.e., they can still pay).

859 **accedam:** "I will approach," or "let me approach." Lycus grovels on his knees in front of Hanno and Agorastocles. A more easily understood word order would be *ego obsecro te per tua genua*.

835 ANTE. Qui tibi lubidost, opsecro, Antamoenides,

    loqui inclementer nostro cognato et patri?

    nam hic noster pater est; hic nos cognovit modo

    et hunc sui fratris filium. ANTA. Ita me Iuppiter

    bene amet, bene factum! gaudeo et volup est mihi,

840 si quidem quid lenoni optigit magni mali,

    cumque e virtute vobis fortuna optigit.

    AG. Bonum virum eccum video, se recipit domum;

    rapiamus in ius. HA. Minime. AG. Quapropter? HA. Quia

    iniuriarum multo induci satius est.

5.6 & 5.7 [original lines 1338–1422, with cuts]

Lycus appears and is immediately confronted by Agorastocles and Hanno, who will bring him to court if they don't get the girls. Antamoenides also wants his girl, but he takes it out on Lycus physically to show that he means it. Everyone wins except the pimp and perhaps Agorastocles, since, as the play ends, Adelphasium is still spurning his advances.

845 LY. Decipitur nemo, mea quidem sententia,

    qui suis amicis narrat recte res suas;

    nam omnibus amicis meis idem unum convenit,

    ut me suspendam, ne addicar Agorastocli.

    AG. Leno, eamus in ius. LY. Opsecro te, Agorastocles,

850 suspendere ut me liceat. HA. In ius te voco.

    LY. Quid tibi mecum autem? HA. Quia hasce aio liberas

    ingenuasque esse filias ambas meas;

    eae sunt surruptae cum nutrice parvolae.

    LY. Iam pridem equidem istuc scivi, et miratus fui,

855 neminem venire qui istas adsereret manu.

    AG. Duplum pro furto mihi opus est. LY. Sume hinc quid lubet.

    HA. Et mihi suppliciis multis. LY. Sume hinc quid lubet:

    collo rem solvam iam omnibus quasi baiolus.

    accedam. per ego te tua genua obsecro

861 **quando…ut:** *quando* usually means "when," but it can also mean "since." Because *addecet* ("it is fitting") is indicative, *ut* must be translated as "as."

862 **faciatis…subveniatis:** The subjunctive can be used as a polite command. *subvenio:* "to support," "to relieve" takes the dative.

    supplici: *supplex, supplicis,* m., "suppliant."

863 **consulam:** future, "I shall deliberate." It introduces an indirect question.

    par…sit: "it is equal," "it is right," like *aequum est* in lines 231 and 779.

865 Antamoenides now joins Hanno and Agorastocles in demanding justice (in his case, his money back) from the pimp.

    inter negotium: Lycus would like to avoid the soldier by claiming that he's already busy. *inter* can mean "during," "in the course of," "occupied with."

866 **nervum:** *nervus, -i,* m., "heavy weight put on the neck."

    abducere: present passive indicative (= *abduceris*), not an infinitive.

867 **faxint:** = *fecerint*; sometimes the perfect subjunctive is used in wishes: "may the gods grant better things (than that)!"

    cenabis foris: "you'll eat out," i.e., you'll be dining in prison.

868 **aurum, argentum, collum:** are in apposition with *tres. aurum* is Agorastocles' Philippic coins (see the note on line 25) that Lycus got when Collybisca entered Lycus' house. *argentum* is Antamoenides' *mina* of silver (line 232), which he paid Lycus even before he arrived on stage.

    tris: = *tres*, accusative plural.

869–871 If Hanno decides to take Lycus to court, he will have to do so in a foreign city (Calydon) under laws and procedures foreign to him. He thus decides, with his daughters' help (lines 872–873), that any delays caused by prosecuting Lycus are not worth the effort.

869 **egomet:** an intensive form of *ego*.

870 **ulcisci:** is the present infinitive of *ulciscor*, "to get revenge on."

    litis: *lis, litis,* f., "law case," "lawsuit."

871 "with all that I've heard of what its (the town's) nature and habits are."

872 Adelphasium and Anterastilis successfully urge Hanno to make peace with the pimp.

    quid…cum istoc rei sit: is an idiomatic way of saying "I have to deal with him."

    rei: partitive genitive after *quid*.

873 **ausculta:** *ausculto, -are,* "to listen to (and obey)" takes the dative.

    diiunge: *dis* ("apart") + *iungo* ("join") means "to separate," "undo," "dismantle."

874 **sis:** = *si vis*, "please." *mereo, -ere, merui, meritum,* "to merit," "to act so as to deserve."

875 **non experiar tecum:** "I'm not going to go to court with you."

876 Agorastocles pretends that he will be kind to the pimp after he gets out of the stocks (*ex nervo*), but he finishes his sentence, "May you be thrown into jail (*in carcerem*)!"

877 Lycus is used to this kind of action from Agorastocles.

    soles: *soleo, -ere,* "to be accustomed."

    tibi me purgatum volo: Antamoenides now apologizes to Hanno for his earlier boorish behavior; see the note at line 834. *se purgare* is "to clean oneself," i.e., "to apologize," "to make amends."

878 **iratus:** translate as "in anger."

879 **uti:** = *ut*.

860 et hunc, cognatum quem tuum esse intellego:

quando boni estis, ut bonos facere addecet

faciatis, vestro subveniatis supplici.

AG. Quid mihi par facere sit, ego mecum consulam.

omitte genua. LY. Mitto, si ita sententia est.

865 ANTA. Heus tu leno! LY. Quid lenonem vis inter negotium?

ANTA. Vt minam mi argenti reddas prius quam in nervum abducere.

LY. Di meliora faxint! ANTA. Sic esto: hodie cenabis foris.

aurum, argentum, collum, leno, tris res nunc debes simul.

HA. Quid me in hac re facere deceat egomet mecum cogito.

870 si volo hunc ulcisci, litis sequar in alieno oppido,

quantum audivi ingenium et mores eius quo pacto sint.

ADE. Mi pater, ne quid tibi cum istoc rei sit pessumo, obsecro.

ANTE. Ausculta sorori. abi, diiunge inimicitias cum improbo.

HA. Hoc age sis, leno. quamquam ego te meruisse ut pereas scio,

875 non experiar tecum. AG. Neque ego; si aurum mihi reddes meum,

leno, quando ex nervo emissus es … compingare in carcerem.

LY. Iamne autem ut soles? ANTA. Ego, Poene, tibi me purgatum volo.

si quid dixi iratus advorsum animi tui sententiam,

id uti ignoscas quaeso; et cum istas invenisti filias,

880 **mihi voluptatist:** = *voluptati est*, another double dative construction. The subject of the verb is the entire *cum*-clause of line 879.

881 **facito:** another future imperative, "make sure that you..." Also in line 885.

882 Lycus tries to calm his angry soldier with another prostitute, but Lycus is not pleased. A *tibicina* is a "flute-player" and the ancients customarily puffed out their cheeks while playing (making them look like the late great trumpeter, Dizzy Gillespie); hence the joke in line 883, where Antamoenides claims not to know whether the girl's breasts or cheeks are bigger. Plautus has Lycus offer this flute-girl for a few last laughs. Given his recent troubles, Lycus would have been hard-pressed to find a good prostitute for Antamoenides. He probably looked around the stage and picked the first slave girl he saw, who would have been the flute-girl providing the musical accompaniment for the play. This is not Lycus' slave, so in effect Lycus would be up to his old tricks of trying to get out of trouble by giving something that's not his to give.

nil moror: "I don't care about..."

883 **nescias:** second-person singular subjunctive addressed, just as it would be in English, to no one in particular: "you couldn't tell..."

buccae...mammae: "cheeks" and "breasts."

884 **cura:** "take care," "make sure."

aurum cras: Lycus now turns to Agorastocles and promises payment the next day. Recall that Agorastocles had done this to the *advocati* too in Act 3.6.

886 **ego vero sequor:** Antamoenides follows Lycus into the brothel, hoping at last to get what he's been denied throughout the play.

887 **quando hinc ire cogitas Carthaginem:** "When are you planning to go from here to Carthage?" Calydon is definitely "backwoods" in comparison to the "big city" of Carthage, and Agorastocles plans to return with Hanno to the place of his birth.

888 **mi ... certum est:** "it is certain for me," "I've decided." See line 257.

ubi primum: "as soon as."

ilico: "immediately."

889 Before leaving, Agorastocles must sell his house, and this will take a few days.

hic: "here."

aliquot: "a few," an indeclinable adjective modifying *dies.*

890 **age sis:** "Come, please," "come on, then." Agorastocles leads his father and his cousins offstage.

891 **PRAECO. Plaudite!:** The whole cast traditionally called for applause at the end of a Roman comedy. If that seems odd to us, it is roughly the equivalent of our curtain call or "Applause" cue cards for TV studio audiences, just more direct. This showed the audience that everything was definitely over and allowed the cast to play with the audience one last time. We decided that the *praeco*, our "bouncer-announcer," would jokingly threaten the audience should they fail to applaud. He had come onstage at line 832 doubling as Agorastocles' tough.

880 ita me di ament, mihi voluptatist. **HA.** Ignosco et credo tibi.

ANTA. Leno, tu autem amicam mihi des facito aut mihi reddas minam.

LY. Vin tibicinam meam habere? **ANTA.** Nil moror tibicinam;

nescias, utrum ei maiores buccaene an mammae sint.

LY. Dabo quae placeat. **ANTA.** Cura. **LY.** Aurum cras ad te referam tuum.

885 **AG.** Facito in memoria habeas. **LY.** Miles, sequere me.

ANTA. Ego vero sequor.

AG. Quid ais, patrue? quando hinc ire cogitas Carthaginem?

nam tecum mi una ire certum est. **HA.** Vbi primum potero, ilico.

AG. Dum auctionem facio, hic opus est aliquot ut maneas dies.

890 **HA.** Faciam ita ut vis. **AG.** Age sis, eamus, nos curemus.

PRAECO. Plaudite!

Appendix

Original "Punic" Lines from *Poenulus*

Following are the original "Punic" lines of the *Poenulus* as recorded in the 1905 OCT, reprinting 1940. The long passages 930–939 and 940–949 are not imitated in our text or on our videotape. They were replaced with some "ad-libbed" English as a segue from the Introduction to Act 5 into the body of Act 5. Our Hanno begins Act 5, line 538 of our text (OCT line 950), in Latin.

930 [Ythalonimualonuthsicorathisymacomsyth
    chymlachchunythmumysthyalmycthybaruimysehi
    liphocanethythbynuthiiadedinbynuii
    bymarobsyllohomalonimuybymysyrthoho
    bythlymmothynnoctothuulechantidamaschon
935 yssidobrimthyfel yth chyl ys chon chem liful
    yth binim ysdybur thinnochotnuagorastocles
    ythemanethihychirsaelychotsithnaso
    bynnyydchilluchilygubulimlasibitthym
    bodialytheraynnynuyslymmonchothiusim]
940 Ythalonimualoniuthsicorathiisthymhimihymacomsyth
    combaepumamitalmetlotiambeat
    iulecantheconaalonimbalumbar dechor
    bats...hunesobinesubicsillimbalim
    esseantidamossonalemuedubertefet
945 donobun.huneccilthumucommucroluful
    altanimauosduberithemhuarcharistolem
    sittesedanecnasotersahelicot
    alemusdubertimurmucopsuistiti
    aoccaaneclictorbodesiussilimlimmimcolus

The rest of the "Punic" lines are conversational, most of them used in gag lines from Milphio who mistranslates the "Punic" by using similar sounding Latin words. This is the idea we played off with our English/Punic against Milphio's understandable, but ludicrous Latin.

Our line number (OCT number)	Punic line	Our version of the line
575, 581, 584 (941, 998, 1001)	avo	"Halo." "Hello."
577–78 (995)	annobynmytthymballebechaedreanech.	"Mother of Baal! This one speaks a little Carthaginian! I'm Hanno. I'm from Carthage."
581 (998)	donni.	"Don't know much Punic, do you?"
585 (1002)	meharboeca.	"Maybe you could help me…"
591 (1010)	muphursa…miuulechianna.	"My reason for…My friend's kid"
594 (1013)	lechlachananilimniichot.	"Look! Can you stop being such a nuisance."

Our line number (OCT number)	Punic line	Our version of the line
598 (1023)	muphonnimsycorathim.	"Oh crap. I suppose I'll just speak to you in Latin "

(A couple of other lines of original Punic were either edited or altered in our version of this scene.)

Another bit of Punic occurs in an exchange between one of Hanno's *pueri* and Giddenis the nurse, who turns out to be the boy's mother. We changed the character of the exchange to suit the silliness of the sudden, unexpected reunion of mother and son.

694 (1144–42)	Puer. avonesilli	Puer. "Mommy!"
	GI. havonbanesilliimustine	GI. "Baal be praised!
	mepsietenestedumetalannacestimim	It's my boy."

Our last change of "Punic" to English was Milphio ordering around the Carthaginian slaves.

701 (1152)	MI. lachanna vos	Go vos

Oral Exercises

Quot cognati tibi sunt?

A.   Fill in the blanks with the appropriate singular or plural noun form.

>   **Sample:** Habeo unam <u>matrem</u>. Heather habet duas **matres**.

1.   Est mihi unus <u>frater</u>. Sunt tibi tres _____.

2.   Habeo duas <u>sorores</u>. Iulius habet unam _____.

3.   Non habeo <u>filium</u>. Mea mater habet quinque _____.

4.   Currit mea <u>germana</u>. Curruntne tuae _____?

5.   Ludo cum mea <u>sorore</u>. Ludisne cum tuis _____?

6.   Dico "I in malam crucem!" meo <u>fratri</u>. Dicis "Ite in malam crucem!" tuis

>   _____.

7.   Amicae <u>sororis</u> meae sunt stultae. Amicae _____ tuarum sunt

>   stultae.

Omnes in familia

B.   Fill in the blanks with the appropriate singular or plural noun form.

>   **Sample:** Meretrix lenonem non amat. Meretrices **lenones** non amant.

1.   Video servum meum. Vides tuos quattuor _____.

2.   Filia mea vivit. Vivuntne _____ vestrae?

3.   Sum liberta. Marcus est _____.

4.   Volo esse civis. Multi servi volunt esse _____.

5.   Amo ancillam meam. Amas _____ tuas.

6.   Nutrix curat pueros puellasque. Puellas puerosque curant _____.

7.   Erus imperat servo. Eri imperant multis _____.

8.   Dominus suae familiae est erus. Eri sunt domini suarum _____.

9.   Iocos dico de ero meo. Iocos dicitis de vestris _____.

Vestis hominem facit

C.   Add the correct form of an adjective to describe the preceding noun.
>   Adjectives to use: purpurus, longus, pulcher, brevis, turpis.

(amiculum, -i: cloak, mantle. tunica, -ae: tunic. vestis, -is, f.: clothing.)

Sample: Odi meum amiculum **purpurum**. Amo tunicas **breves**.

1. Gero amiculum _____.
2. Gerimus amicula _____.
3. Eius vestis est _____.
4. Habetis tunicas _____.
5. Quis est ille vir cum tunica _____?
6. Marcus pretium non amat tunicarum _____.

Ecce odium meum

D. Add the correct form of an adjective to describe the preceding noun.
Adjectives to use: scelestus, stultus, turpis, audax.

   Sample: Non video tuum servum **stultum**.

1. Es furcifer _____!
2. Non sumus advocati _____.
3. Servio ero _____.
4. Gratias non ago haruspici _____.
5. Latrones _____ odi.
6. I in malam crucem, o miles _____!

Quales sunt dramatis personae?

E. Choose a subject from list A and an adjective from list B; then create a sentence
by adding a form of the verb "to be" (esse). Make sure that the adjective agrees
with the noun(s)!

List A	List B
leno	cupidus
miles	scelestus
servi	callidus
nutrix	Poenus
advocati	tardus
Adelphasium	pudicus
Agorastocles	stultus
Giddenis et Milphio	turpis
Adelphasium et Hanno	felix
leno et miles	demens
Adelphasium et Anterastilis	pauper

Aphrodisia

F.   Fill in the blanks with the proper form of the verb given in parentheses.
(**Teachers:** This exercise can be done in any tense; it is particularly useful for
practicing the use of the perfect and imperfect.)

Ego et soror ad aedem Veneris _____ (venio). Multi ibi _____

(adsum), quia deam _____ (propitio, colo) volebant. Bonus odor turis

aedem _____ (compleo). Sacerdos primum hostiam ad aram _____

(duco). Nos in pompa _____ (sequor, ambulo). Deinde, nos omnes

hostiam immolatam _____ (video). Tandem sacerdos hostiam _____

(sacrifico). Servi sacerdotis hostiam _____ (incido) et haruspex exta

_____ (inspicio). _____ (clamo) hic "Exta optima _____ (sum)!"

Nos _____ (gaudeo) quia sacerdos _____ (lito); dea irata non

_____ (sum). Coquus carnem hostiae _____ (coquo) et nos omnes

_____ (edo) et vinum _____ (bibo).

Periculum sub luna

G.   Fill in the blanks with the proper form of the relative pronoun (*qui, quae,
quod*). You will need to read the whole sentence before deciding what case,
number, and gender to choose.

Adelphasium meretrix, _____ (whom) in matrimonium ducere voluit

Agorastocles, peregrinum pulchrum clam adamavit. Nemini nisi sorori,

_____ (who) quoque amatorculos habebat, hoc dixit. Hic peregrinus,

_____ (whom) Adelphasium amavit, erat miles e castris Lejeuniaticis.

Adelphasium omni nocte e domo, in _____ (which) cum sorore patreque

vivebat, exibat. Illi ambulabant sub luna, _____ (which) vias monstrabat,

et multa dicebant de suis vitis, _____ (which) una agere voluerunt.

Nocte quadam hi duo ambulaverant ad portam, _____ (which) amatoribus

erat loco amoeno. Idem autem erat locus sordidus _____ (which)

frequentabant praedones mali. Unus ex his praedonibus nostram

Adelphasium eiusque amatorculum, _____ (who) praedonibus visi sunt

divites, conspexit. Clam suos convocavit amicos, _____ cum (with whom)

coepit petere amatores. Miles, _____ (whose, to whom) animus erat

imbecillus, exclamavit fugitque. Agorastocles autem, _____ (who) dormire

non potuerat, forte ambulabat per portam et cucurrit ad Adelphasium et

operam dedit. Gladio transfixit omnes praedones, _____ (whose) cordia

plena vitiorum erant, per cerebrum.

Agorastocles spectavit Adelphasium, _____ (to whom) dixit "Meum

corculum, te amo. Volo te in matrimonium ducere. Te servavi ab istis

_____ (who) te petiverunt. Nonne sum ille _____ (whom) ames?" Sed

Adelphasium ei misero dixit "Gratias tibi ago, Agorastocles, sed te non amo."

Quid et quocum cenas?

H.   Oral questions. Use the vocabulary listed with exercises I–L to ask and answer
      questions about meals and eating.

1. Potasne aquam? lac? vinum?
    Quid potat X (i.e., a student's
    name)?

2. Potatisne vinum domi? cum
    parentibus?

3. Quid potavisti hodie?

4. Mavisne panem an caseum?
    Mulsa an salsa? Sesumam an
    frictas nuces?

5. Quota hora cenas? prandes?
    ientas?

6. Cenas cum familia?

7. Amasne coquere?

8. Quid coquis? Cui coquis?

9. Editne familia tua cibum
    quem coquis? Edisne tu ipse?

10. Quis tuae familiae coquit?
    Coquitne bene an male?

Heri aliqua emi, et foeda erant!

I.   Create a dialogue about shopping for food.

      In the ancient world, shopping at the market was usually done by men. It is

      not unlikely, therefore, that Milphio was the one who bought the food that he

      enjoyed so much onstage. In pairs, have a conversation between Milphio and a

      merchant in which Milphio chooses various foods and haggles over the price.

Aut ede aut gere!

K. Antamoenides, our *miles*, goes to the local *popina* for some refreshment after being rejected by Anterastilis. Construct a dialogue in groups of two or three, taking the roles of the *miles*, the *puer*, and (optionally) the cook. Possibilities: nothing seems to suit the *miles*; the *puer* spills everything; the food's too hot or too cold (à la Goldilocks); the *puer* doesn't speak Latin; the *miles* gets food poisoning; the *puer* turns out to be Antamoenides' long-lost brother; the *miles* gets drunk.

Constitutum

L. Agorastocles and Adelphasium go on a date to the *popina*. Construct a dialogue between Agorastocles, Adelphasium, and the waiter. (Who pays? Who eats what? Do Agorastocles and Adelphasium even like each other? Do they both behave decently? Does the waiter bring the right food? Are there other customers? Is this their first date?)

Vocabulary for Exercises I–L

people

agricola, -ae, m. farmer
mercator, -oris, m. merchant
coquus, -i, m. cook
puer, -i, m. waiter (Romans had no waitresses, only waiters.)
emptor, -oris, m. customer
constitutum, -i, n. date

places and things

taberna, -ae, f. shop, stall
macellum, -i, n. food market
forum, -i, n. open downtown area used as a market and a gathering-place
popina, -ae, f. greasy-spoon restaurant, dive, cafeteria
culina, -ae, f. kitchen
latrina, -ae, f. restroom
mensa, -ae, f. table
linteum, -i, n./mappa, -ae, f. napkin
coclear, -aris, n. spoon

culter, -tri, m. knife
furcilla, -ae, f. fork
poculum, -i, n. glass, cup
patella, -ae, f. dish, plate
catillus, -i, m. bowl

food and cooking

cibus, -i, m. food
lac, lactis, n. milk
vinum, -i, n. wine
aqua, -ae, f. water
panis, -is, m. bread
caseus, -i, m. cheese
mel, mellis, n. honey
sesuma, -ae, f. sesame seed
papaver, -eris, n. poppy seed
triticum, -i, n. flour
oleum, -i, n. olive oil
frictae nuces, -arum -um, f. pl. roasted nuts
laterculi, -orum, m. flat pastries
circulus, -i, m. doughnut
crustulum, -i, n. cookie

holus, holeris, n. vegetable(s)
puls, pultis, f. porridge
sal, salis, m. salt
caro, carnis, f. meat
bubula, -ae, f. beef (bos, bovis, m./f. bull, cow)
agnina, -ae, f. lamb (agnus, -i, m. lamb; ovis, ovis, m./f. sheep)
porcina, -ae, f. pork (porcus, -i, m./ porca, -ae, f. pig)
piscis, -is, m. fish
gallina, -ae, f. chicken (gallus, -i, m. rooster)
frustum, -i, n. piece, slice
esurio, -ire, —, -itum to be hungry
sitio, -ire, —, — to be thirsty
ientaculum, -i, n. breakfast
prandium, -i, n. lunch
cena, -ae, f. dinner
edo (es, est, edimus, estis, edunt), esse, edi, esum to eat
iento, -are to eat breakfast
prandeo, -ere, prandi, pransum to eat lunch
ceno, -are to eat dinner
friget it's cold
calet it's hot
tepet it's lukewarm
tepescit it's cooling off
tabula, -ae, f. menu
relinquo, -ere, reliqui, relictum to leave
in furno in the oven
peruro, -ere, -ussi, -ustum to burn
furnus non valet the oven is broken
lignum nobis deest we're out of wood
devoro, -are to gulp down
bibo, bibere, bibi, —/poto, -are to drink
effundo, -ere, effudi, effusum to spill
ructo, -are to belch

aegroto, -are to be sick
venter, -tris, m. stomach
vomo, -ere, vomui, vomitum to barf

service

eheu! Oops!
doleo/paenitet me Sorry!
amabo (te)/sis/quaeso please
gratias tibi ago thank you
faciam alterum? Should I make another one?
gratis dabo I'll give (it) (to you) for free
tardus, -a, -um/lentus, -a, -um slow
piger, -gra, -grum/segnis, -e lazy, sluggish
festino, -are/propero, -are/maturo, -are to hurry
ede aut exi! Eat (it) or leave!
exspecto (duas horas) I've been waiting (for two hours) (the acc. shows duration of time)
peto, -ere, -ivi, -itum aliquid ab aliquo to order something from someone
fero, ferre, tuli, latum to bring
refer! Bring it back!
obliviscor, -i, oblitus sum to forget (+ genitive or accusative)

swears and insults

i in malam crucem! Go to the devil! Go jump off a cliff! (more or less)
di te perdant! May the gods destroy you! Damn you!
mastigia, -ae, m. whipping boy, rascal, scoundrel, scum
vappa, -ae, m. dullard, lame-brain
nebulo, -onis, m. low-life
codex, -icis, m. blockhead, fool
(me)hercle golly (gee), gosh
numquam reveniam! I'll never come back!

money and payment

pecunia, -ae, f. money
argentum, -i, n. silver
aurum, -i, n. gold
nummus, -i, m. coin
vilis, -e cheap
carus, -a, -um expensive
nimium carus, -a, -um too expensive
   (*nimium* is an adverb)
quanti stat/stant ... ? How much
   does/do ... cost? (*quanti* is the
   genitive of unspecified price)

stat quattuor nummis It costs four
   coins (*nummis* is the ablative of
   specific price)
capiam! I'll take it!
pendo, -ere, pependi, pensum to pay
bene/male emo (emere, emi, emptum)
   to buy at a good/bad price
pendo alicui aliquid pro aliquo to pay
   someone something for something
stips, stipis, f. tip
rationem sis! (Bring the) check, please!
computemus Let's settle the bill.

Vita servae

M. You are telling a new friend the story of your life. Your history is very similar to that of Adelphasium and Anterastilis. Read aloud the dialogue below.

Amica: Ubi habitabas, quando eras puella parva?

Tu: Quando puella parva eram, Carthagini habitabam.

Amica: Libera eras?

Tu: Libera quidem et laeta, sed praedo malus me surripuit cum nutrice et

sorore.

Amica: Quid tum factum est?

Tu: Misera eram. Non poteram invenire patrem et matrem, quia praedo me

vendidit et facta sum serva! Non iam libera eram.

Amica: Doleo. Crudelisne tuus est erus? Vapulasne?

Tu: Felix sum, quia dominus meus non nimium crudelis est. Sed non lutum

est lutulentius isto domino!

Amica: Vera dicis. Fersne onera?

Tu: Non fero; meretrix sum. Erus autem meus me tenet castam, quia me

vendere vult. Si virgo et pura ero, erus meus plus pecuniae recipiet.

Amica: Erisne semper meretrix?

Tu: Nolo. Volo libertatem emere.

Amica: Si liberta esses, quid faceres?

Tu: Civis fierem, et corculo meo nuberem. Deinde matrem patremque invenirem, et lenonem scelestum interficerem!

N. Based on the dialogue above (M), tell a friend about your own experience as one of the slaves in the play (Milphio, Collybisca, Syncerastus, Giddenis, Adelphasium, Anterastilis). To help you tell your story, have your friend ask you some of the following questions, and make up others.

> Quo modo te tractat erus tuus?
>
> Dic mihi de ero tuo. Qualis homo est?
>
> Sunt tibi multi labores? Quales labores fers?
>
> Cogitasne emere libertatem?
>
> Quando eris libertus/liberta?

---

people

erus, -i, m./era, -ae, f. master/mistress

leno, -onis, m. pimp

servus, -i, m./serva, -ae, f. slave, servant

nutrix, -icis, f. nurse

vilicus, -i, m. overseer, manager

ancilla, -ae, f. maid

familia, -ae, f. household (including the slaves)

status

liber, -a, -um free

libertus, -a, -um freed (from slavery)

ingenuus, -a, -um free-born

civis, -is, m./f. citizen

libero, -are to free (someone)

manumitto, -mittere, -misi, -missum to free (one's own slave)

relations

tracto, -are to treat

cogito, -are to plan, intend, think (about)

vapulo, -are to get a beating, to be beaten

verbero, -are/ferio, -ire, —, — to strike, lash, hit

servio, -ire, -ivi, -itum to serve, be a servant (+ dative)

iubeo, -ere, iussi, iussum to order, command (+ accusative and infinitive)

enslavement

emo, -ere, emi, emptum to buy

vendo, -ere, vendidi, ventum to sell

surripio, -ere, surripui, surreptum to steal

praedo, -onis, m. pirate

captivus, -i, m. prisoner of war

Exta sola sciunt

O. Pretend that you are a *meretrix* or *adulescens* or *servus* or *ancilla* or *matrona*, and that you want the *haruspex* to read your fortune from the entrails of an animal. The *haruspex* demands a payment for Aphrodite. (The money somehow ends up in his own pocket.) The fortune he tells you is directly related to how much money you give: the more money he gets, the more glorious his predictions become. In pairs, produce several variations based on the examples below. Use your school textbook and the *Poenulus* glossary to create answers in which each word begins with the same letter.

Samples

Tu: Quid portendunt mihi exta?

Haruspex: Da, domina, deae decem drachmas.

Tu: Sed non habeo. Leno omnem pecuniam tenet meam.

Haruspex: Cave! Currus compescet crura cras.

Tu: Quid portendunt mihi exta?

Haruspex: Da, domina, deae decem drachmas.

Tu: Habeo tantum quinque drachmas.

Haruspex: Fortasse fies felix; fortasse frustra fugies fatum foedum.

---

more vocabulary

portendo, -ere, -i, portentum to
    foretell, portend
exta, extorum, n. pl. entrails
drachma, -ae, f. a Greek coin

Esne mater mea?

P1.   Describe your family to a friend. Use the questions below to get started.
P2.   Describe your ideal family to a friend, using contrafactual conditions ("If my father were ninety years old, I'd ..."). Use the questions below to get started.

mater, -tris, f. mother
pater, -tris, m. father
soror, -oris, f./germana, -ae, f. sister
frater, -tris, m./germanus, -i, m. brother
filius, -i, m. son
filia, -ae, f. daughter
avus, -i, m. grandfather
avia, -ae, f. grandmother
canis, -is, m./f. dog
felis, -is, m./f. cat

Quot sorores/fratres habes?

Quot annos natus est pater?

Quis filiorum est maximus natu?

Quis est minimus natu?

Iurgasne cum fratribus? Cum parentibus?

Habitatne tecum avus/avia/frater/soror?

Cenatne tota familia uno tempore?

De quo loquimini cenantes?

   de re publica, ludo, officio, libris, novis, amicis

Quis habet curam rei familiae? Cui est familia curae?

Quis cibum emit et parat?

Quis mundat domum tuam?

Quis lavat vasa?

Quis lavat vestes?

Quis herbas secat?

Sermo cottidianus

Q.   Practice everday chit-chat with a partner, or make up your own small talk based on the following short models.

In via

A.   Salve!

B.   Salve atque tu.

A.   Quid agis (rei)?

B.   Ego me moror; nugas ago. Et tu?

A.   Omne in ordine. Vale!

B.   Et tu vale.

Cognitio

A.   Salve!

B.   Et tu edepol, quisquis es.

A.   Quid est nomen tibi?

B.   Agorastocles sum. Et quid tibi est nomen?

A.   Hanno sum, patruus tuus. Mecum veni domum.

B.   O mi patrue, faciam ita ut vis. Eamus; nos curemus.

Sorores

Anterastilis: Soror, cur nullos habemus amatorculos?

Adelphasium: Nescio, soror, sed stulta es magis quam volo.

Anterastilis: Immo vero callida sum. Linguam compescas!

Adelphasium: Et tu tace. Quid mihi molesta es, obsecro?

Glossary

A

a, ab	+ abl.	from, by, away from
abduco, -ere, -duxi, -ductum		to lead away, take away, take off
abeo, -ire, -i(v)i, -itum		to go away, depart
abstineo, -tinere, -tinui, -tentum		to abstain, refrain, keep off
absumo, -ere, -psi, -ptum		to use up, waste, destroy, carry off
abutor, -uti, -usus sum	+ acc.	to use up, exploit
ac		and
accedo, -ere, -essi, -essum		to draw near, approach
accido, -ere, -i		to fall down, descend; occur, happen
accuro, -are		to take care of, provide for
acerbus, -a, -um		bitter, cruel, harsh
Acheruns, Acheruntis, m. or f.		the underworld, the land of the dead
actutum		at once, immediately
ad	+ acc.	towards, to, for
addecet, -ere	impers.	it is fitting, it is proper
addico, -ere, -ixi, -ictum		to assign, hand over
addo, -ere, -idi, -itum		add, attach, apply
adduco, -ere, -uxi, -uctum		to bring (on, in), lead (in)
Adelphasium, -ii, f.		the heroine, a prostitute loved by Agorastocles
adeo		moreover, besides; (w. *neque*) in fact
adeo, -ire, -i(v)i, -itum		to approach, go towards
adfero, adferre, attuli, allatum		to bring
adfleo, -ere, -evi, -etum		to weep (in accompaniment)
adhibeo, -ere, -ui, -itum		to use, employ, bring in, introduce
adicio, -icere, -ieci, -iectum		to cast; to direct; to add; (w. *animum*) to consider
adlego, -are (allego, -are)		to commission, employ
adlicio, -licere, -lexi, -lectum		to entice, attract, win over
adludio, -are		to play along
admodum		very much; exactly
adopto, -are		to adopt
adporto, -are		to bring in (news)
adsero, -ere, -ui, -tum		to lay claim to someone (w. *liberali manu*)
adsimulo, -are		to pretend, imitate
adstringo, -ere, -xi, -ctum		to bind; to implicate (in crime)
adsum, -esse, -fui	+ dat.	to be present; to help out
adulescens, -ntis		young, youthful; a young person
adveho, -vehere, -vexi, -vectum		to carry, convey
advena, -ae, m. or f.		foreigner, visitor from abroad
advenio, -venire, -veni, -ventum		to come to, arrive at, reach
adversus	+ acc.	against
advocatus, -i, m.		legal assistant
advorsum		see *adversus*
advorto, -ere, -ti, -sum		(w. *animum*) to pay attention, notice
aedes, -is, f.		temple, shrine; (pl.) house
aedilis, aedilis, m.		aedile (Roman official in charge of public games)

aegre	with difficulty, barely, scarcely
Aegyptini, -orum, m.	Ethiopians
aequus, -a, -um	equal, level, just, fair
aes, aeris, n.	copper, bronze; anything made of copper or bronze
aetas, aetatis, f.	age, period of time, lifetime
Aetolus, -a, -um	of Aetolia (a region in NW Greece)
affatim	(*ad + fatim*) sufficiently
Africanus, -a, -um	of Africa, African
Africus, -a, -um	of Africa, African
agnus, -i, m.	lamb
ago, agere, egi, actum	to do, act, drive, treat, give (thanks), go
Agorastocles, -is, m.	the rich young man in love with Adelphasium
aha	(an expression of surprise)
aio, ais, ait, aiunt; aibat (3 sing. impf.)	to say, declare
ala, -ae, f.	wing
alacer, -cris, -cre	nimble, quick, eager
alium, ali(i), n.	garlic
alius, -a, -um	(an)other
alicarius, -a, -um	connected with porridge (*alica*)
alienus, -a, -um	belonging to another; foreign; strange
aliquis, -quid	someone, something
aliquot	a certain number, some
alius, -a, -ud	(an)other
alo, -ere, -ui, -tum	to foster, nourish, sustain, support
alter, -a, -um	(an)other; the other (of two)
alumna, -ae, f.	foster daughter
amabilitas, -tatis, f.	attractiveness
amatio, -onis, f.	love-making
amator, -oris, m.	lover (man)
amatorculus, -i, m.	little lover, "lover boy"
amatrix, -icis, f.	lover (woman)
ambo, -ae, -o	both
ambulo, -are	to walk
amiculum, -i, n.	outer garment, cloak, skirt
amicus, -a, -um	friendly, well-disposed; friend, girl- or boyfriend
amitto, -mittere, -misi, -missum	to release, let slip, pass over
amo, -are	to love [*amabo* (*te*) = please; *amo* (*te*) = thanks]
amor, -oris, m.	love, passion
amplector, -cti, -xus sum	to embrace
amplexor, -ari	to embrace
Ampsigura, -ae, f.	Agorastocles' mother
an	or; (introduces a surprised question)
Anactorium, -ii, n.	a town in NW Greece
ancilla, -ae, f.	maid, attendant, female slave
animus, -i, m.	soul, spirit, nature; courage
annus, -i, m.	year
Antamoenides, -is, m.	the soldier interested in Anterastilis
antehac	beforehand, previously, before now
Anterastilis, -is, f.	a prostitute, Adelphasium's sister
Antidamas, Antidamae, m.	Hanno's Calydonian friend (now dead)

antiquus, -a, -um		old, old-fashioned
anulatus, -a, -um		decked out with rings, beringed
apage!		Off! Away with (you)!
Aphrodisia, -orum, n.pl.		the festival of Aphrodite
appareo, -ere, -ui, -itum		to appear, be visible, be around
apparo, -are		to prepare, plan
appello, -are		to call, summon
appono, -nere, -sui, -situm		to place near, set down
apscedo, -ere, -essi, -essum		to depart, go away
apsumo, -ere, -psi, -ptum		see *absumo*
apud	+ acc.	at or in the house of; among; in the presence of
aqua, -ae, f.		water
aquilus, -a, -um		dark
ara, -ae, f.		altar
arbiter, -tri, m.		witness, judge
arbitrario		doubtfully
arbitror, -ari		to think, judge, consider
arcesso, -ere, -ivi, -itum		to summon, fetch, gather
area, -ae, f.		a place (for a bird-catcher to set his snares)
argentum, -i, n.		silver; money
arte		closely, tightly
asinus, -i, m.		ass, donkey
aspicio, -spicere, -spexi, -spectum		to behold, look at, view
asto, -are, -iti		to stand by, stand still
at		but
ater, -tra, -trum		black, dark
atque		and
atriensis, -is, m.		steward, major-domo
atritas, -tatis, f.		blackness, darkness
attat		(expression of surprise) Ah! Yow!
Atticus, -a, -um		of Attica, Attic, Athenian
attinet, -ere, attinuit	impers.	it pertains, it is relevant, it matters
attrecto, -are		to touch, handle (abusively)
auctio, -onis, f.		auction, public sale
auctor, -oris, m.		an authority, an advocate, supporter
audacter		audaciously, bravely
audeo, audere, ausus sum		to dare
audio, -ire, -ivi, -itum		to hear, listen to
aufero, auferre, abstuli, ablatum		to carry off, do away with
aureus, -a, -um		golden, made of gold; golden (coin)
auricula, -ae, f.		ear
auris, -is, f.		ear
aurora, -ae, f.		dawn
aurum, -i, n.		gold
ausculto, -are		to listen
aut		or
autem		on the other hand, indeed, however, in fact
autumo, -are		to allege, claim, say
auxilium, -ii, n.		help, assistance
avarus, -a, -um		greedy

avis, -is, f.	bird

B

baiolus, -i, m.	porter, carrier
balineum, -i, n.	public bathhouse
ballista, -ae, f.	ballista, catapult
ballistarium, -ii, n.	place where a *ballista* is set up
basilice	in a regal manner, royally
bellus, -a, -um	pretty
bellulus, -a, -um	(dim. of *bellus*) cute, sweet
bene	well
benigne	kindly, amicably
benignitas, -tatis, f.	kindness
bestia, -ae, f.	beast
bibo, bibere, bibi	to drink
bisulcis, -e	forked
blandidicus, -a, -um	sweet-talking, smooth-tongued
blandior, -iri	to coax, sweet-talk
blandus, -a, -um	smooth-talking
bonus, -a, -um	good, nice, pleasant
bracchialis, -e	pertaining to the arms
bubulus, -a, -um	made of ox hide
bucca, -ae, f.	mouth

C

cado, -ere, cecidi, casum		to fall
cadus, -i, m.		jar
caedo, -ere, cecidi, caesum		to cut, kill
caelum, -i, n.		sky, heaven
caenum, -i, n.		mud, filth
calidus, -a, -um		warm, hot
calleo, -ere		to be experienced, skilled, crafty
callidus, -a, -um		experienced, crafty, sly
calx, calcis, m. or f.		heel
Calydonius, -a, -um		of Calydon, a city in Aetolia
canalis, -is, m. or f.		channel, canal; materials to construct a channel
canis, -is, m. or f.		dog
capio, capere, cepi, captum		to take hold of, seize, grasp
capto, -are		to seek; to catch or seize in a crafty way
caput, capitis, n.		head
carcer, carceris, m.		prison
careo, carere, carui, caritum	+ abl.	to lack, be without
carnufex, carnuficis, m.		executioner, hangman
Carthago, Carthaginis, f.		Carthage
Carthaginiensis, -e		Carthaginian
caseus, -i, m.		cheese
cassus, -a, -um		hollow, empty; useless
castellum, -i, n.		castle, fort, citadel
castra, -orum, n.pl.		camp

castus, -a, -um		morally pure, spotless, virtuous
cate		intelligently, craftily
catus, -a, -um		intelligent, crafty
cauponius, -a, -um		of a shopkeeper or innkeeper
causa, -ae, f.		cause, reason; lawsuit
causa	+ gen.	for the sake of
caveo, cavere, cavi, cautum		to beware of, take care
cedo		tell (imperative)
celeber, celebris, celebre		honored by an assembly, crowded; famous
celeriter		swiftly
celo, -are		to hide away, keep secret
cena, -ae, f.		meal
ceno, -are		to eat a meal, dine
censeo, -ere, censui, censum		to think, suppose, believe
centiens		a hundred times
cerebrum, -i, n.		brain
cerno, -ere, crevi, cretum		to see
certus, -a, -um		certain, sure; established, true
cervus, -i, m.		stag, deer
ceterus, -a, -um		other
Chius, -a, -um		Chian, of Chios, an island in the Aegean
chlamydatus, -a, -um		wearing a military cloak (*chlamys*)
cinaedus, -i, m.		a passive homosexual; "fag"
circumduco, -ere, -duxi, -ductum		to cheat, deceive
circus, -i, m.		an oval arena for horseraces and other sports
cito		quickly, speedily, soon
civis, -is, m. or f.		citizen
clam		secretly
clanculum		secretly, privately
clienta, -ae, f.		female client
clueo, -ere		to be named, called, spoken of
clunis, -is, m. or f.		buttock
cochlea, -ae, f.		snail
cogito, -are		to consider, reflect upon, think
cognatus, -i, m.		relative
cognosco, cognoscere, cognovi, cognitum		to recognize, know
colaphus, -i, m.		a punch with the fist
collum, -i, n.		neck
Collybisca, -ae, f.		Collybisca, Agorastodes' female estate manager
colo, -ere, colui, cultum		to cherish, care for, protect
comicus, -a, -um		pertaining to comedy
comitium, -ii, n.		place where the Roman assembly meets
commemini, -isse		to remember
commode		duly, properly; well, skilfully
commoditas, -tatis, f.		advantage, benefit; pleasantness
commodus, -a, -um		fit, suitable, friendly to
commonstro, -are		to show, point out something fully
comparo, -are		to compare
compello, -are		to address
compello, -ere, compuli, compulsum		to drive together to a place, move, incite

compendium, -ii, n.	shortening, sparing, a saving in anything done
comperco, -ere, compersi	to save up
compesco, -ere, compescui	to curb, restrain
compingo, -ere, compegi, compactum	shut up (in prison), confine
complector, complecti, complexus sum	to embrace
compleo, -ere, complevi, completum	to fill up
complexus, -us, m.	an embrace
compono, -ere, composui, compositum	to devise, invent, conspire to make
comprobo, -are	to show or verify that something is good
concesso, -are	to stop from, cease from
concilio, -are	to provide, prepare
condigne	very worthily
condisco, -ere, condidici	to learn carefully
condoceo, -ere, condocui, condoctum	to train, instruct
confero, conferre, contuli, collatum	to unite, join; to bring together for comparison; to compress, condense
coniector, coniectoris, m.	interpreter, soothsayer
conlaudo, -are	to praise very highly
conlibertus, -i, m.	fellow freedman
conlino, -ere, conlevi, conlitum	to make dirty, pollute
consanguinei, -orum, m.pl.	relatives
consequor, consequi, consecutus sum	to follow after, accompany
consilium, -ii, n.	plan
consisto, -ere, constiti, constitum	to stop, halt
consulo, -ere, consului, consultum	to consult with
contemplor, contemplari, contemplatus sum	to gaze at, behold
contemptim	scornfully
continuo	immediately
contero, -ere, contrivi, contritum	to wear down; to treat contemptuously
contrecto, -are	to touch, fondle
convenio, -ire, conveni, conventum	to be proper, suitable; to meet
converto, -ere, converti, conversum	to change, turn
conviva, -ae, m. or f.	companion for dinner or drinking
copia, -ae, f.	opportunity, resource
copulo, -are	to join together, unite, have sex
coqua, -ae, f.	female cook
cor, cordis, n.	heart, mind
corbita, -ae, f.	cargo ship, barge
cordate	wisely
cordolium, -ii, n.	sorrow, grief
corius, -ii, m.	skin, hide; leather whip
corpus, corporis, n.	body
corruptela, -ae, f.	enchantment, source of seduction
cortina, -ae, f.	bucket
cras	tomorrow
cratis, -is, f.	wicker basket or caging
credo, -ere, credidi, creditum	to believe, trust, entrust
creo, -are	to produce, make
crepo, -are	to rattle, creak, rustle; to fart
crucio, -are	to torture, torment, distress

crudus, -a, -um		rough, cruel
Crurifragius, -a, -um		"broken-legged"
crux, crucis, f.		a cross; *i in malam crucem* go hang yourself, go to the devil
culpa, -ae, f.		fault, defect
cupido, cupidinis, f.		desire, passion
cupio, -ere, cupivi, cupitum		to desire, wish, want
cur		why
cura, -ae, f.		care, concern
curo, -are		to care for, attend to, take care
curro, -ere, cucurri, cursum		to run
cursim		quickly, hastily
cursor, cursoris, m.		runner
cursus, -us, m.		the action of running; speed

D

damnum, -i, n.		harm, injury, loss
de	+abl.	from; about, concerning
dea, -ae, f.		goddess
deamo, -are		to be desperately in love with
debeo, -ere, debui, debitum		to owe; to 'ought'
decet, decuit		it is fitting, it is proper
decipio, -ere, decepi, deceptum		to catch, entrap, deceive
defero, deferre, detuli, delatum		to bring to
deglubo, -glubere, -glupsi, -gluptum		to skin, flay
dehinc		from here; from this time
delecto, -are		to please, amuse
delicia, -ae, f.		delight, pleasure, charm
delubrum, -i, n.		temple, shrine
demens, dementis		mad; foolish
demonstro, -are		to show, point out
denego, -are		to reject, refuse, deny
dens, dentis, m.		tooth
denuo		again
depingo, -ere, depinxi, depictum		to depict, represent by painting
despondeo, -ere, despondi, desponsum		to promise a woman in marriage
detrudo, -ere, detrusi, detrusum		to force, drive down
deus, -i, m.		god
deveho, -ere, devexi, devectum		to sail off with
devello, -ere, develli, devolsum		to pluck out hair/feathers
devoro, -are		to swallow, gulp down
dexter, -a, -um		the right-hand side
di		= *dei* (nom. or voc. pl. of *deus*)
dico, -ere, dixi, dictum		to speak, say
dictum, -i, n.		that which is said, an utterance
dierecte		(adverbial form of *dierectus*)
dierectus, -a, -um		(an uncertain term of dismissal)
dies, diei, m.		day
Diespiter, Diespitris, m.		an archaic form of *Iuppiter*

differo, differre, distuli, dilatum		to confound, bewilder, distract
digitus, -i, m.		finger
dignus, -a, -um		worthy
diiungo, -ere, diiunxi, diiunctum		to sever, break off
dilido, -ere		to batter to pieces
diobolaris, -e		priced at two obols (very cheap)
diripio, -ere, diripui, direptum		to tear to shreds; to rob, loot
disco, -ere, didici		to learn
dispendium, -ii, n.		expense, cost
disperdo, -ere, disperdidi, disperditum		to destroy or ruin utterly
diu		for a long time
dives, divitis		wealthy; rich person
divido, -ere, divisi, divisum		to divide up
divinus, -a, -um		divine, religious
do, dare, dedi, datum		to give
doceo, -ere, docui, doctum		to teach, instruct
docte		cleverly; learnedly
doleo, -ere, dolui, dolitum		to be in pain, be sad
dominus, -i, m.		master
domus, -i (also domus, -us), f.		home
dono, -are		to give a gift, reward
donum, -i, n.		gift
dubito, -are		to be in doubt
dubius, -a, -um		doubtful
duco, -ere, duxi, ductum		to lead; to marry; to consider, believe, think
ductito, -are		to be in the habit of taking someone home
dudum		just now; for a long time (up to the present)
dulcis, -e		sweet; dear, agreeable
dulciculus, -a, -um		sweet little
dum		while, until
duo, duae, duo		two
duplus, -a, -um		double in size or quantity

E

e		see *ex*
eampse		see *ipse*
ecastor		By Castor!
eccam		Here she (it) is!
ecce	+ acc.	Behold! Look!
eccum		Here he (it) is!
ecquis, ecquid		Is there anyone who? Is there anything that?
ecfero, ecferre		see *effero*
ecficio, -ere		see *efficio*
edo, esse, edi, esum		to eat
edentulus, -a, -um		toothless
edepol		By Pollux!
effero, efferre, extuli, elatum		to lift, raise
efficio, -ere, effeci, effectum		to accomplish
efflictim		passionately

egenus, -a, -um		requiring assistance, needy
ego		I
egomet		I (the -*met* adds emphasis)
egredior, egredi, egressus sum		to go/come out
eheu		alas
eho		Hey you!, What?!
elego, -ere, elegi, electum		to select, choose out
eloquor, eloqui, elocutus sum		to say, speak
em	+ acc.	Here you are!, Look at this!
emitto, -ere, emisi, emissum		to free
emo, emere, emi, emptum		to buy
enico, -are		to deprive of life, kill
enim		for
eo, ire, i(v)i, itum		to go
eo		to there, for that purpose
epulae, -arum, f. pl.		sumptuous meal, banquet
eques, equitis, m.		cavalryman, member of the equestrian order
equidem		indeed
ergo		therefore
eripio, eripere, eripui, ereptum		to snatch away
erro, -are		to wander around, err
erus, -i, m.		master
estur		(from *edo*) eating goes on, people eat
et		and
etiam		also, even
eu		Fine!, Splendid! (often ironic)
euge		Oh good!, Fine!
eunuchus, -i, m.		eunuch
evado, -ere, evasi, evasum		to go/come out
evenio, -ire, eveni, eventum		to happen, come about; to turn out
evoco, -are		to call out, summon
ex, e		from, out of; as a result of
excido, -ere, excidi		to fall off, drop out
excrucio, -are		to torture
exemplum, -i, n.		example
exeo, -ire, exii, exitum		to go/come out
exhibeo, -ere, exhibui, exhibitum		to provide, produce
exitium, -ii, n.		destruction, disaster
exorno, -are		to prepare; to decorate, beautify
exoro, -are		to persuade
expalpo, -are		to obtain by coaxing or caressing
expedio, -ire, expedivi, expeditum		to explain
experior, -iri, expertus sum		to go to trial with
expeto, -ere, expetivi, expetitum		to desire
explico, -are		to expand, increase
expolio, -ire, expolivi, expolitum		to polish; to adorn
exspecto, -are		to wait for, hope for
exta, -orum, n.pl.		entrails
extemplo, extempulo		immediately

extra	on the outside
extrudo, -ere, extrusi, extrusum	to force to go out, push away
exturbo, -are	to drive out, remove a thing by force

F

fabre	skillfully
fabrica, -ae, f.	device, trick
fabula, -ae, f.	play, drama
fabulor, -ari, fabulatus sum	to talk, chat
facete	aptly, cleverly; amusingly
facetus, -a, -um	clever
facies; -ei, f.	face; appearance
facilis, -e	easy
facile	easily
facilius	more easily
facinus, facinoris, n.	misdeed, crime
facio, -ere, feci, factum	to do, make
factum, -i, n.	deed
fallacia, -ae, f.	trick
falsus, -a, -um	false
familia, -ae, f.	household
fanum, -i, n.	shrine, temple
farferum, -i, n.	coltsfoot (a plant)
fateor, -eri, fassus sum	to admit, acknowledge
fatim	see *affatim*
fel, fellis, n.	bile, gall; bitterness
fere	about, approximately; virtually, nearly
ferio, -ire	to strike, beat
ferme	see *fere*
fero, ferre, tuli, latum	to carry, bear; to endure
festino, -are	to hasten, hurry
festivus, -a, -um	excellent, fine; witty, amusing
festus, -a, -um	(with *dies*) holiday in honor of a god
fides, -ei, f.	faith
fiducia, -ae, f.	guarantee, assurance
filia, -ae, f.	daughter
filius, -ii, m.	son
fingo, -ere, finxi, fictum	to change, transform, modify, rearrange
fio, fieri, factus sum	to become; to happen, go on
flagitium, -ii, n.	a shameful act, outrageous conduct
folium, -ii, n.	leaf
foras	out from within, out of doors
foris	outside, out of doors
foris, -is, f.	door
forma, -ae, f.	appearance
formido, -are	be afraid of, fear, dread
formido, formidinis, f.	terror, alarm
fortasse	perhaps
forte	by chance

fortiter	bravely
fortuna, -ae, f.	fortune
fortunatus, -a, -um	fortunate, lucky
fovea, -ae, f.	pit
frango, -ere, fregi, fractum	to break
frater, fratris, m.	brother
frico, -are, fricui, frictum	to smooth or polish; to rub clean
frigefacto, -are	to make cold
frugi (indeclinable adj.)	having merit or worth, honest
fugio, -ere, fugi	to flee
fugitivus, -i, m.	runaway slave
funda, -ae, f.	leather strap for shooting stones; sling
fundito, -are	to shoot at with slings
fur, furis, m.	thief, robber
furcifer, furciferi, m.	villain, scoundrel
furtim	secretly, stealthily
furtivus, -a, -um	obtained by theft, stolen
furtum, -i, n.	robbery, theft
fustis, -is, m.	stick, club

G

gaudeo, -ere, gavisus sum	to be delighted, happy
gaudium, -ii, n.	joy, delight
gens, gentis, f.	clan, family, group of people, nation
genu, -us, n.	knee
genus, generis, n.	type, character, class
germana, -ae, f.	sister
gero, -ere, gessi, gestum	to carry, bear, perform, do
gestito, -are	to be in the habit of carrying
gestus, -us, m.	posture, gesture, motion
Giddenis, Giddenenis, f.	Hanno's maid
globus, -i, m.	ball, sphere
gnatus, -a, -um	born; (as noun) child
gnosco, -ere, novi, notus	to know, get to know
gradus, -us, m.	step, walk
gralator, -oris, m.	stilt-walker
grandiculus, -a, -um	biggish, diminutively large
grassor, -ari	to roam, prowl
gratia, -ae, f.	grace, favor; (pl., with *ago* and *habeo*) thanks
gratus, -a, -um	grateful, appreciative
gugga	(uncertain term of abuse)

H

habeo, -ere, habui, habitum	to have, keep, consider; (w. *gratias*) to offer thanks
habito, -are	to live, reside, dwell
habitus, -us, m.	condition; attitude, style, character
hahahae	A-hah!
halagora	(uncertain term of abuse)
hallex, hallecis, f. or n.	fish sauce sediment, or the big toe

Hanno	Agorastocles' Carthaginian uncle
hariolus, -i, m.	soothsayer, prophet
haruspex, -icis, m.	soothsayer, prophet
hau, haud	not at all, in no way
hem	(expresses surprise)
hercle	(expresses mild surprise or emotion)
heri	yesterday
heus	Hey! (calls attention)
hic	here; at this point
hic, haec, hoc	this (person, thing)
hinc	from here, from this point
hirquinus, -a, -um	like a goat, goatish
hodie	today
homo, hominis, m.	human being
honestus, -a, -um	reputable, honorable
honor, -oris, m.	honor, respect, esteem
hospes, -itis, m.	guest; host
hospitalis, -e	connected with hospitality
hospitium, -ii, n.	hospitality
hostia, -ae, f.	sacrificial animal
huc	hither, to here
humanus, -a, -um	human

I

Iahon, -onis, m.	Agorastocles' father
iam	now; already; further
ianua, -ae, f.	door
ibi	there
ibidem	in the same place
idoneus, -a, -um	suitable, apt
igitur	therefore, then
ignarus, -a, -um	ignorant
ignavus, -a, -um	sluggish, lazy
ignosco, -ere, ignovi, ignotum + dat.	to forgive
ilico	on the spot, immediately
ille, illa, illud	that; the; he, she, it
illic	there, in that place
illic, illaec, illuc	(=*ille, illa, illud* + *-ce*; cf. *hic, haec, hoc*)
illim	thence, from there
illinc	(=*illim* + *-ce*) thence, from there
immo	(introduces a correction) on the contrary
immodestus, -a, -um	immoderate, uncontrollable
immolo, -are	to sacrifice
immortalis, -e	immortal
impero, -are	to give orders
impetro, -are	to get what one wants by asking
impono, -ere, imposui, impositum	to put on, place on top
improbus, -a, -um	unchaste, lewd, shameless
in	(+ abl.) in, on; (+ acc.) into, against

incedo, -ere, incessi, incessum	to walk, move
incesto, -are	to defile, pollute
incitae, -arum, f.pl.	(w. *redigere*) to "checkmate"
inclementer	rudely, harshly
incommodus, -a, -um	annoying, troublesome
inde	from there
indignus, -a, -um	unjust, undignified, shocking
indo, indere, indidi, inditum	to put in, insert
induco, -ducere, -duxi, -ductum	to take (to court); (w. *animum*) to bring oneself (to do something)
industria	(in phrase *ex industria*) diligently, deliberately
infelico, -are	to bring bad luck upon
infelix, -icis	unlucky, ill-fated
infortunium, -ii, n.	misfortune, trouble
ingenium, -ii, n.	character
ingenuus, -a, -um	free-born
inibi	in that place; in that situation
inimicitia, -ae, f. (usu. pl.)	unfriendly relations, a state of enmity
inimicus, -a, -um	unfriendly, inimical; (subst.) enemy
iniuria, -ae, f.	injustice, a wrong, injury
iniuste	unjustly
inlex, -icis, m. or f.	enticer, one who allures
innatus, -a, -um	innate, inborn
inopiosus, -a, -um	lacking, bereft of (+ gen.)
inquam, inquis, inquit	to say
inrideo, inridere, inrisi, inrisum	to laugh at, make fun of, mock
inridiculum, -i, n.	laughingstock
inrigo, -are	drench; refresh (with liquid)
insidiae, -arum, f.pl.	trap, ambush
insignite	in a striking manner
insipientia, -ae, f.	stupidity, folly
insisto, -ere, institi	to press on, proceed
inspecto, -are	to look at, observe, examine, watch
insperatus, -a, -um	unhoped-for
inspicio, -spicere, -spexi, -spectum	to inspect
insto, -are, institi	to stand over, loom, threaten
insulsus, -a, -um	uninteresting, boring, dull
insum, -esse, -fui	to be within
intellego, -legere, -lexi, -lectum	to understand
intendo, -ere, intendi, intentum	to tense; to point (a weapon at), aim
inter + acc.	between, among
interficio, -ficere, -feci, -fectum	to kill
intereo, -ire, -i(v)i, -itum	to perish
interim	in the meantime, meanwhile
interpres, -pretis, m.	interpreter, translator
interrogo, -are	to question, ask
intro	indoors (moving indoors from outside)
intus	within, inside
invenio, -venire, -veni, -ventum	to find, discover
invenustus, -a, -um	not charming, unattractive

invidia, -ae, f.	ill-will, envy
invitus, -a, -um	unwilling(ly)
iocor, -ari	to joke, make a joke, jest
iocus, -i, m.	joke; (*per iocum*) as a joke, jokingly
ipse, -a, -um	him-, her-, itself; (as adj.) very
ipsus	archaic form of *ipse*
ira, -ae, f.	anger, rage
iracundus, -a, -um	angry
iratus, -a, -um	angry, angered
ire	see *eo*
is	"you go" (*ire*); "he" or "with them" (*is, ea, id*)
is, ea, id	he, she, it; that, those
isdem, eadem, idem	the same (person, thing)
iste, ista, istud	he, she, it; that, those
istinc	from over there, from where you are
ita	thus, in that way, so
itaque	(and) so
item	likewise, in the same manner
iterum	again, once more
itidem	likewise, similarly
iubeo, -ere, iussi, iussum	to command, order
Iuno, Iunonis, f.	Juno, queen of the gods, Jupiter's wife
Iuppiter, Iovis, m.	Jupiter, king of the gods, Juno's husband
iuro, -are	to swear an oath, take an oath
ius, iuris, n.	law; (*in ius*) to court
iustus, -a, -um	just, right
iuventus, -tutis, f.	the youth, young men as a group

L

labellum, -i, n.	lip
lacrumo, -are	to cry, weep
laevus, -a, -um	left, on the left
lapis, lapidis, m.	rock, stone
latebra, -ae, f.	hiding-place, den, lair
laterculus, -i, m.	pastry shaped like a brick (*later, lateris,* n.)
Latine	in Latin
latro, -are	to bark, howl (at)
latro, -onis, m.	mercenary solider; brigand, robber
latrocinor, -ari	to serve as a mercenary soldier
laudo, -are	to praise
lautus, -a, -um	washed; fine, respectable
lavo, -are, lavi, lautum	to wash
lectus, -i, m.	bed
legio, -onis, f.	legion (a large unit of the army)
leniter	without exertion; gently, mildly
leno, -onis, m.	pimp
lenullus, -i, m.	little pimp, "pimple"
lenunculus, -i, m.	little pimp
lepide	agreeably, delightfully, charmingly

lepidus, -a, -um		agreeable, delightful, charming
Leucadius, -a, -um		from Leucas, an island in the Aegean Sea
levis, -e		light, insubstantial, trivial
lex, legis, f.		law
liber, -era, -erum		free
liberalis, -e		pertaining to freedom; see *adsero*
libere		freely
liberi, -orum, m.pl.		children (of either sex)
libero, -are		to set free
liberta, -ae, f.		freedwoman (formerly enslaved)
libertas, -tatis, f.		freedom
libertinus, -i, m.		freedman
libertus, -i, -m.		freedman, (formerly enslaved)
licet, licere, licuit	impers.	it is permitted
ligula, -ae, f.		spoon; (an uncertain term of abuse)
lingua, -ae, f.		tongue, language
lippitudo, -inis, f.		bleariness, watering of the eyes
lis, litis, f.		lawsuit
lito, -are		to obtain favorable omens from a sacrifice
locus, -i, m.		place; position
longus, -a, -um		long
loquor, loqui, locutus sum		to speak, say
loripes, -pedis		having deformed feet
lubet, lubere, lubuit		it is pleasing; (w. *mihi*) I like
lubido, -inis, f.		desire, urge
lucrum, -i, n.		profit, money
ludificatus, -us, m.		teasing; an object of ridicule
ludificor, -ari		to play with, trifle with
ludo, -ere, lusi, lusum		to play
ludus, -i, m.		game, sport; (pl.) public games
lupus, -i, m.		wolf; pimp
luteus, -a, -um		muddy, grimy
lutulentus, -a, -um		muddy, grimy
lutum, -i, n.		mud
Lycus, -i, m.		the pimp (his name means "wolf" in Greek)
lymphaticus, -a, -um		frenzied, mad, crazy

M

macero, -are	to soak, steep; to vex, wear down
macto, -are	to harass, punish
maena, -ae, f.	a small fish, used by the poor as food
magis	more (adv.); rather
magnus, -a, -um	great, big, large
maior, maius	(comp. of *magnus*) greater, larger, older
maiusculus, -a, -um	slightly older
mala, -ae, f.	cheek
male	wickedly, awfully, poorly
maledictum, -i, n.	insult, verbal abuse
malevola, -ae, f.	female enemy

malitia, -ae, f.	wickedness
malo, malle, malui	to prefer
malum	trouble, evil, harm
malus, -a, -um	bad, evil, wicked
mamma, -ae, f.	breast
mammeatus, -a, -um	big-breasted
mando, -are	to entrust, give as a command
mane	in the morning
maneo, manere, mansi, mansum	to remain, stay
manifesto, -are	in the act, undeniably
manstruca, -ae, f.	sheepskin coat (a term of abuse)
manto, -are	to wait for, await
manufestus, -a, -um	caught in the act, caught red-handed
manus, -us, f.	hand
mare, maris, n.	ocean, sea
Mars, Martis, m.	Mars, the god of war
marsuppium, -ii, n.	pouch, moneybag
mas, maris	male, manly, virile
mastigia, -ae, m.	whipping boy, rascal, scoundrel
mater, -tris, f.	mother
maxumus, -a, -um	(superl. of *magnus*) greatest, biggest
mecastor	by Castor! (an oath used by women)
medicus, -a, -um	doctor
medius, -a, -um	middle; in the middle of
mel, mellis, n.	honey
melior, melius	(compar. of *bonus*) better
memini, meminisse	to remember
memoria, -ae, f.	memory, recollection
memoro, -are	to say, mention
mendax, -acis	lying, untruthful
mensis, -is, m.	month
mens, mentis, f.	mind
mentior, -iri, mentitus sum	to lie
mercator, -oris, m.	merchant, salesman
mercatus, -us, m.	market, fair
mercennarius, -i, m.	mercenary soldier, hired worker
mereo, -ere, meruisse, meritum	to earn, deserve
meretricius, -a, -um	pertaining to prostitutes
meretrix, -icis, f.	prostitute
merito	deservedly, rightly
meruleus, -a, -um	colored like a blackbird (*merula, -ae*, f.)
merus, -a, -um	pure, absolute
metuo, -ere, metui	to fear, be afraid of
meus, -a, -um	my
migdilix	(uncertain term of abuse)
miles, militis, m.	soldier
militaris, -e	of the army; (*aes militare*) soldier's pay
mille (pl. *milia*)	thousand
Milphio, -onis, m.	Agorastocles' crafty slave
miluus, -i, m.	a bird of prey

mina, -ae, f.	a unit of weight, about a pound
minus	less
minusculus, -a, -um	slightly smaller (younger)
miror, -ari, miratus sum	to be amazed, surprised
miser, -era, -erum	poor, wretched
miseria, -ae, f.	distress, affliction, misery
mitto, -ere, misi, missum	to let go
modeste	modestly, discreetly
modicus, -a, -um	ordinary, moderate-sized
modo	now, just now; simply, just
modo	(*quo modo*) how
modus, -i, m.	moderation; manner, way
moechus, -i, m.	adulterer
mola, -ae, f.	mill
molestus, -a, -um	annoying
molliculus, -a, -um	soft, tender, delicate
monstro, -are	to point out, show, report
monstrum, -i, n.	monster, horrible creature
mora, -ae, f.	delay
mordeo, -ere, memordi, morsum	to bite
moror, -ari, moratus sum	to remain, wait; to delay, cause to wait
mortalis, -e	mortal
mos, moris, m.	manner, custom, way; morals, character
mox	soon
mulier, mulieris, f.	woman
mulsus, -a, -um	honey-sweet
multus, -a, -um	much, great, many
munditer	cleanly, neatly
munditia, -ae, f.	elegance, cleanliness
mundo	(*in mundo*) ready, in store, in readiness
muriaticum, -i, n.	pickled fish
murrinus, -a, -um	of myrrh
mus, muris, m. or f.	mouse
muto, -are	to change
Mytthumbalis, Mytthumbalis, m.	Hanno's father

N

nam	for, since
narro, -are	to tell, relate
natura, -ae, f.	nature, character
navis, navis, f.	ship
ne	truly, for sure (w. *edepol*)
ne	not, lest (w. purpose clauses and commands)
-ne	(asks a question); (intensifies a pronoun)
nec	and not
necesse (neuter adj.)	necessary
neco, -are	to kill, slay, destroy
nego, -are	to deny, refuse, say no, say that . . . not
negotium, -ii, n.	business, occupation; difficulty, trouble

nemo, neminis, m. or f.		no one
nenia, -ae, f.		funeral song, dirge
nequam (indeclinable adj.)		worthless; (*dare, facere nequam*) to make mischief
neque		and not (= *nec*)
nequeo, -ire, nequivi, nequitum		to be unable
nequiquam		in vain
nervus, -i, m.		prisoner's chain; "the stocks"
nescio, -ire, nescivi, nescitum		not to know, to be ignorant
neve		and not, nor
nex, necis, f.		murder, slaughter
ni		if not, unless
nihil (nil), n.		nothing
nihilo minus		none the less, just the same
nihilum, -i, n.		nothing
nimbatus, -a, -um		trifling, frivolous
nimis		too much, excessively
nimium, -ii, n.		too much, excess
nimius, -a, -um		excessive, too great
nisi		if not, unless, except
nobilis, -e		known, famous
nolo, nolle, nolui		not to wish, to be unwilling
nomen, nominis, n.		name
non		not
nonne		(interrogative, expects yes for an answer)
nos		we, us
nosco, -ere, novi, notum		to know, recognize (someone)
noster, nostra, nostrum		ours
nox, noctis, f.		night
noxia, -ae, f.		fault, offence
nubes, nubis, f.		cloud
nugae, -arum, f. pl.		nonsense; *agere nugas* to play the fool
nullus, -a, -um		no (as an adjective)
num		(interrogative, expects no for an answer)
numeratus, -a, -um		counted out
numero		too soon, untimely
numerus, -i, m.		number
nummus, -i, m.		a Roman silver coin
numnam		(stronger form of *num*)
numquam		never
numquid		Is there anything? (expects "no" for an answer)
nunc		now
nunciam		right now, this very moment
nuntio, -are		to announce, make known, inform
nutrix, nutricis, f.		nurse
nux, nucis, f.		nut

O

O		(+ voc. or acc.) Oh!
ob	+ acc.	on account of

obicio, -ere, obieci, obiectum		to hold out, put before
oblecto, -are		to delight, please, amuse
obnoxius, -a, -um	+ dat.	subject to, obligated to
oboedio, -ire, oboedivi, oboeditum	+ dat.	to obey, be obedient to
obsecro, -are		to beseech, implore, beg
obsequor, obsequi, obsecutus sum	+ dat.	to gratify
obviam		readily available; (w. verb motion) to meet
occasio, occasionis, f.		an occasion, opportunity, good moment
occido, -ere, occidi, occisum		to kill
occipio, -ere, occepi, occeptum		to begin
ocior, ocius		faster
oculus, -i, m.		eye
odi, odisse		to hate
odium, -ii, n.		hatred, disgust
odor, odoris, m.		smell, scent, odor
Oedipus, -i, m.		Oedipus, the legendary king of Thebes known for many unfortunate things (unknowingly killing his father and sleeping with his mother), who in the happier early days of his career solved the riddle of the Sphinx.
offa, -ae, f.		bite, morsel
offero, offerre, obtuli, oblatum		to bring, cause
officium, -ii, n.		job, official duty
oleo, -ere, olui		to emit a smell, smell of (anything)
oleum, -i, n.		olive oil
omitto, -ere, omisi, omissum		to let go
omnis, -e		all, every
onerarius, -a, -um		carrying freight
onus, oneris, n.		load, burden
opera, -ae, f.		work, labor, care, attention, help
operio, -ire, operui, opertum		to cover
opinor, -ari, opinatus sum		to think, believe, suppose, imagine
opiparus, -a, -um		rich, splendid, sumptuous
oportet, -ere, oportuit	impers.	it is necessary, proper; one ought
oppidum, -i, n.		town
opportune		opportunely, at just the right time
opsecro, -are		see *obsecro*
opstipesco, -ere, opstipui		to be astounded, amazed
optingo, -ere, optigi		to happen, occur
optimus, -a, -um		(superl. of *bonus*) best
optume		most wonderfully
opturbo, -are		to disturb, throw into confusion
opus, operis, n.		(*opus est*) there is need of
oratio, orationis, f.		speech
orator, oratoris, m.		spokesman, ambassador
ordo, ordinis, m.		order, line
oriundus, -a, -um		born, originating in
ornatus, -us, m.		clothing, dress
orno, -are		to adorn, decorate
oro, -are		to beg, beseech

os, oris, n.		mouth
os, ossis, n.		bone
ostendo, -ere, ostendi, ostentum or -sum		to show, display
ostreatus, -a, -um		striped like an oyster; rough, scabby

P

pactum, -i, n.		agreement; means, manner, method
pactus, -a, -um		arranged by negotiation, agreed
paenitet, -ere, paenituit	impers.	to give reason for complaint or regret; to be sorry
pallium, -ii, n.		outer garment
palumbes, -is, m. or f.		pigeon; fool, sucker
Panamanicus, -a, -um		Panamanian, of Panama
panis, -is, m.		bread
papaver, papaveris, m. or n.		poppy, poppy-seed
par, paris		equal; fair, reasonable
parco, -ere, peperci (also parsi)	+ dat.	to refrain from (an action); to be merciful
parens, parentis, m. or f.		a parent, relative
paro, -are		to provide; to get; to make preparations for
pars, partis, f.		part
parvolus, -a, -um		small, tiny
pater, patris, m.		father
patior, pati, passus sum		to allow (something to happen), put up with
patria, -ae, f.		fatherland
patritus, -a, -um		belonging to one's father
patronus, -i, m.		patron, advocate in court
patruelis, -is, m. or f.		(w. *frater* or *soror*) cousin on the father's side
patruissimus, -i, m.		comic superlative of *patruus* – "uncliest one"
patruus, -i, m.		a father's brother, paternal uncle
paucus, -a, -um		few
pauper, pauperis		poor; poor person
pauperculus, -a, -um		poor little
pausa, -ae, f.		intermission, pause
pax, pacis, f.		peace
peccatum, -i, n.		error; moral offence
pecto, -ere, pexi, pexum		to thrash
pedes, peditis, m.		foot-soldier
pedica, -ae, f.		shackle
peiiero, -are		to swear a false oath, perjure
peiiurus, -a, -um		that has broken an oath, perjured
peior, peius		(compar. of *malus*) worse
pendeo, pendere, pependi, pensum		to value; (w. *nihili*) to disregard
penes	+ acc.	so far as concerns, on the part of
per	+ acc.	through; by (in oaths); by means of
percontor, -ari, percontatus sum		to question, investigate
perdo, -ere, perdidi, perditum		to destroy
perdoceo, -ere, perdocui, perdoctum		to teach, instruct
perduco, -ere, perduxi, perductum		to lead; to bring over by persuasion
peregrinus, -a, -um		foreign, alien
pereo, -ire, perii, peritum		to perish, die

perfacilis, -e		very easy
pergo, -ere, perrexi, perrectum		to continue
pergraecor, -ari		to behave like a Greek (to party hard)
perhibeo, -ere, perhibui, perhibitum		to regard, consider
periculum, -i, n.		danger, risk
perniger, pernigra, pernigrum		very black
perpetuo		continuously, constantly
perspicio, -ere, perspexi, perspectum		to become aware, recognize
perspisso		very slowly
pessumus, -a, -um		(superl. of *malus*) worst
Philippeus, -a, -um		see *Philippus, -a, -um*
Philippus, -i, m.		gold coin
Philippus, -a, -um		connected with a gold coin
pictor, pictoris, m.		painter
pietas, pietatis, f.		attitude of respect toward gods, parents, etc.
piget, pigere, piguit	impers.	to cause revulsion or displeasure
pignus, pignoris, n.		anything given as a security, token
pingo, -ere, pinxi, pictum		to paint
pinna, -ae, f.		feather
pistor, pistoris, m.		baker, miller
placo, -are		to make favorably disposed, appease
plaga, -ae, f.		a violent blow
plane		clearly
plaudo, -ere, plausi, plausum		to clap, applaud
plebeius, -a, -um		belonging to the plebeian (lower) class
plenus, -a, -um		full
ploratillus, -a, -um		inclined to weep, tearful
pluma, -ae, f.		feather
plumbeus, -a, -um		made of lead, heavy
plurumus, -a, -um		very many
plus, pluris, n.		more, a greater amount
podagrosus, -a, -um		affected with gout
Poenus, -a, -um		Punic, Carthaginian
pol		By Pollux!
polio, -ire, polivi, politum		to polish
polliceor, -eri, pollicitus sum		to promise
pollicitor, -ari, pollicitatus sum		to promise vigorously
pompa, -ae, f.		parade, ceremonial procession
pone	+ acc.	at or to the back of, behind
popina, -ae, f.		low-class eating house, cook shop
popularis, -is, m. or f.		fellow citizen
popularitas, popularitatis, f.		fellow-citizenship
populus, -i, m.		people
porcus, -i, m.		pig
porro		furthermore, in turn
portendo, -ere, portendi, portentum		to foretell a future event from an omen
porto, -are		to bring with one, carry
portus, -us, m.		port, harbor
posco, -ere, poposci		to ask for, demand
post	+acc.	after

post		afterwards
postea		afterwards
posthac		from now on
postibi		afterwards
postilla		after that time
postulo, -are		to ask for, demand; to expect
potens, potentis		in possession of
poto, -are		to drink
possum, posse, potui		to be able
potissimum		in the best way
potius		rather
praebeo, -ere, praebui, praebitum		to put forward, provide
praeceptum, -i, n.		instruction, order
praecipio, -ere, praecepi, praeceptum		to advise, command, teach
praeco, -onis, m.		bouncer
praeda, -ae, f.		booty
praedico, -are		to make known, declare
praedo, praedonis, m.		one who lives by robbery; a pirate
praepotens, praepotentis		outstandingly powerful
praesens, praesentis		being present
praesentarius, -a, -um		paid on the spot; immediately effective
praesertim		above all, especially
praesidium, -ii, n.		a source or means of security
praesterno, -ere		to scatter in front
praesto, -are, praestiti, praestitum		to excel, be superior to others
praestrigiator, praestrigiatoris, m.		a trickster
praetor, praetoris, m.		a Roman magistrate
prandeo, -ere, prandi, pransum		to have lunch
prandium, -ii, n.		midday meal, lunch
prehendo, -ere, prehendi, prehensum		to take hold of, seize; to arrest
pretium, -ii, n.		reward; *operae pretium esse* to be worthwhile; rank
pridem		some time ago, once; *iam pridem* for a long time
pridie		on the day before
primoris, -e		extremity, the tip of; *digiti primores* fingertips
primum		first, at first
primus, -a, -um		first, foremost, leading
principium, -ii, n.		beginning
prior, prius		ahead, in front of; *prius quam* before
privo, -are		to deprive, rob
pro		(interjection) *pro Iuppiter* good God!
pro	+ abl.	in place of, in return for, in front of
probe		properly; certainly, surely
probrum, -i, n.		digraceful, shameful act
probus, -a, -um		good, honest, virtuous
procedo, -ere, processi, processum		to make one's way, proceed
procul		far away
procuro, -are		to look after, attend to
procus, -i, m.		a suitor's attendant
prodeo, -ire, prodii, proditum		to come forth
prodigus, -a, -um		rich, wealthy

profecto	indeed, truly, certainly
progredior, progredi, progressus sum	to go forth, proceed
prohibeo, -ere, prohibui, prohibitum	to restrain, prevent
promitto, -ere, promisi, promissum	to predict; to promise
promus, -i, m.	steward
propere	hastily, quickly
propero, -are	to hurry, hasten
propitio, -are	to make favorable, appease
propitius, -a, -um	gracious, kind, favorable
propius	nearer, closer
propter + acc.	on account of
propudium, -ii, n.	a shameful act; a vile wretch
proseco, -are, prosecui, prosecatum	to cut away, cut off
proseda, -ae, f.	a common prostitute
proserpo, -ere	to creep forwards, crawl along
proximus, -a, -um	closest, nearest
prurio, -ire	to itch, be eager for
pudet, -ere, puduit, puditum est impers.	to be shameful, disgraceful
pudice	bashfully, modestly
pudor, pudoris, m.	shyness, modesty
puella, -ae, f.	girl, girlfriend
puer, pueri, m.	boy; waiter
pugna, -ae, f.	battle
pugnus, -i, m.	fist
pulcher, pulchra, pulchrum	beautiful, handsome
pulchre	beautifully
pulchritudo, pulchritudinis, f.	beauty
pullus, -i, m.	a young animal; chick
pulto, -are	to beat, strike, knock
Punicus, -a, -um	Carthaginian
Punice	in the Punic language
purgo, -are	to clean
purpurus, -a, -um	purple
purus, -a, -um	clean, pure
puto, -are	to think, believe

Q

quaerito, -are	to keep on looking for, seek, try to obtain
quaero, -ere, quaes(i)i (or -ivi), quaesitum	to seek
quaeso	I beg you; please
quaestus, -us, m.	income
quam	than, as; how
quamquam	although
quando	when
quantillus, -a, -um	how small, how little
quantus, -a, -um	how great, how much, as much as
quapropter	why
quasi	as if, like
qui	how

qui, quae, quod	who, which
quia	because
quidem	certainly, indeed
quiesco, -ere, quievi, quietum	to say nothing more, be quiet
quin	why not; indeed, in fact, actually; but that
quippe	for indeed
quippini	why not
quis, quid	who, what (*quid* = what, why, or how)
quisquam, quicquam	anyone, anything
quisque, quaeque, quidque	each
quisquis, quidquid	whoever, whatever
quivis, quaevis, quodvis	any that you please
quo	to what place, where; (*quo modo*) how
quod	because
quoias, quoiatis	of what country
quoniam	because
quoque	in the same way; also, besides, too
quorsum	in the direction in which
quot	how many

R

rapio, rapere, rapui, raptum	to cause to go along, take forcibly to
recedo, -ere, recessi, recessum	to withdraw, move back or away
recens, recentis	fresh in the mind or memory
recipio, -ere, recepi, receptum	to receive; (as a reflexive) to return
recludo, -ere, reclusi, reclusum	to open a door
recte	in accordance with the truth; properly
reddo, reddere, reddidi, redditum	to return, give back
redeo, -ire, redii, reditum	to come back
redigo, -ere, redegi, redactum	to drive back
refero, referre, rettuli, relatum	to bring back
regio, regionis, f.	region
relinquo, relinquere, reliqui, relictum	to leave behind
reliquia, -ae, f.	the remnants, remains
reliquus, -a, -um	remaining
remex, remigis, m.	rower, oarsman
renuntio, -are	to report
reor, reri, ratus sum	to think, suppose
reperio, -ire, repperi, repertum	to discover
repleo, -ere, replevi, repletum	to fill up
repudio, -are, repudiavi, repudiatum	to reject
res, rei, f.	matter; activity, practice, business; property
respicio, -ere, respexi, respectum	to look back
respondeo, -ere, respondi, responsum	to answer
resto, restare, restiti	to remain, linger
revertor, reverti, reversus sum	to return
revoco, -are	to call back
rex, regis, m.	king
rite	properly, in accordance with ritual

rogo, -are	to ask
Romanus, -a, -um	Roman
rumpo, -ere, rupi, ruptum	to cause to explode; to rupture
rursus	again

S

sacrufico, -are	to perform a sacrifice
saepe	often
saeviter	violently, angrily
salsus, -a, -um	preserved or flavored with salt
saltem	at least
salus, salutis, f.	greeting; savior
saluto, -are	to greet, say hello
salve	Hello!
salvus, -a, -um	safe, unharmed
sampsa, -ae, f.	crushed olive
sane	certainly
sapienter	wisely
sapientia, -ae, f.	wisdom
sapio, ere, sapi(v)i	to be intelligent, show good sense
sarcinatus, -a, -um	loaded with a pack (*sarcina, -ae,* f.)
sarrapis	(uncertain term of abuse)
sat, satis	enough, sufficient
savium, -ii, n.	kiss
scapulae, -arum, f.pl.	shoulder-blades
scelestus, -a, -um	wicked
scilicet	of course
scio, -ire, scivi, scitum	to know
scortum, -i, n.	prostitute
scurra, -ae, m.	clown, fool, wit, "man about town"
secundus, -a, -um	second
secus	otherwise, differently
sed	but
sedeo, -ere, sedi, sessum	to be sitting
sedo, -are	to reduce the violence of, assuage
sedulo	diligently, earnestly
segrego, -are	to separate; (w. *sermonem*) to stop
semel	a single time, once
semen, seminis, n.	race, breed
sementis, -is, f.	sowing
semper	always
sempiternus, -a, -um	everlasting, eternal
sententia, -ae f.	way of thinking, opinion
sentio, -ire, sensi, sensum	to perceive
sequor, sequi, secutus sum	to follow
serio	seriously
serius, -a, -um	important, serious
sermo, sermonis, m.	speech, conversation
serva, -ae, f.	female slave

servio, -ire, servi(v)i, servitum	+ dat.	to be a slave, serve (a master)
servilis, -e		slavish, servile
servola, -ae, f.		slave-girl
servolus, -i, m.		slave-boy
servus, -i, m.		slave
sesuma, -ae, f.		sesame plant or seed
sex		six
sexaginta		sixty
sexennis, -e		six years old
si		if
sic		thus, so
Siculus, -a, -um		Sicilian
sicut		just as, like
signum, -i, n.		distinguishing mark or feature
silex, silicis, m. or f.		rock, stone
simia, -ae, f.		monkey
similis, -e		similar
simul		together; at the same time
sine	+ abl.	without
sino, -ere, sivi, situm		to allow
siquidem		if it is really possible that
sitio, sitire		to thirst, be thirsty
sobrina, -ae, f.		female second cousin
soleo, -ere, —, solitus sum		to be accustomed
solus, -a, -um		alone
sona, -ae, f.		belt
sordeo, -ere		to be dirty, shabby
sordidulus, -a, -um		dirty little, shabby little
soror, sororis, f.		sister
sospes, sospitis		safe and sound
species, speciei, f.		appearance
spectaculum, -i, n.		sight, spectacle
spectator, spectatoris, m.		spectator
specto, -are		to watch
sperno, -ere, sprevi, spretum		to reject with scorn, despise
spero, -are		to hope
Sphinx, Sphingis, f.		Sphinx
spissigradissimus, -a, -um		slowest-moving
spondeo, -ere, spopondi, sponsum		to pledge; to promise in marriage
sponsa, -ae, f.		a woman promised in marriage, fiancée
st		Hush!, Sh!
statura, -ae, f.		bodily height, stature
stella, -ae, f.		star
sterno, sternere, stravi, stratum		to lay out on the ground, spread
strenue		quickly
studeo, -ere, studui		to be eager
stultus, -a, -um		foolish
subdolus, -a, -um		sly, treacherous, sneaky
subigo, -ere, subegi, subactum		to force, compel
subvenio, -ire, subveni, subventum		to come to the support of, help

suffero, sufferre, sustuli, sublatum	to endure
summus, -a, -um	highest
sumo, -ere, sumpsi, sumptum	to put on (clothes)
sumptus, -us, m.	the spending of money, expense, cost
supplex, -plicis, m. or f.	suppliant, one who begs for mercy
supplicium, -ii, n.	punishment
suppono, -ere, supposui, suppositum	to place under or beneath
supremus, -a, -um	most exalted, supreme
surripio, -ere, surripui, surruptum (surptum)	to steal
surrupticius, -a, -um	stolen, kidnapped
suscenseo, -ere, suscensui, suscensum	to be angry or indignant with
suspendo, -ere, suspendi, suspensum	to hang; kill by hanging
suus, -a, -um	his, hers, its, theirs
sycophanta, -ae, m.	swindler, imposter
Syncerastus, -i, m.	a eunuch who works for and hates Lycus

T

taceo, -ere, tacui, tacitum		to be silent
tactio, tactionis, f.		act of touching
taedet, taedere, taesum est	impers.	to tire, bore
tam		to such a degree, so
tamen		nevertheless
tango, -ere, tetegi, tactum		to touch; to deprive fraudently of
tantillus, -a, -um		so small
tantus, -a, -um		so great, so much
tantusdem, tantadem, tantundem		just as great, just as much
tarditudo, tarditudinis, f.		slowness of movement or action
tardus, -a, -um		slow
tempto, -are		to test; to investigate
tempus, temporis, n.		time
tenebrae, -arum, f.pl.		darkness
teneo, -ere, tenui, tentum		to hold or grasp with the mind or body
tergeo, tergere, tersi, tersum		to rub dry
tergum, -i, n.		back
tertius, -a, -um		third
tessera, -ae, f.		token
testimonium, -ii, n.		testimony
testis, testis, m.		witness
tibicina, -ae, f.		female flute player
timeo, -ere, timui		to be afraid
tot		so many
totus, -a, -um		the whole of, all, entire
tragoedus, -i, m.		actor of tragedies
tranquillus, -a, -um		peaceful, calm
trecenti, -ae, -a		three hundred
tres, tria		three
triobolum, -i, n.		a three-obol piece, a coin of small worth
triticum, -i, n.		wheat flour
tu		you (singular)

tum	then
tumultus, -us, m.	commotion
tundo, -ere, tutudi, tunsum	to beat, assail
tunica, -ae, f.	short-sleeved garment worn under the toga
tunicatus, -a, -um	wearing a tunic
turba, -ae, f.	crowd
turpis, turpe	foul, repulsive; shameful, disgraceful
turtur, turturis, m.	turtle-dove
tus, turis, n.	frankincense
tuus, -a, -um	your, yours (singular)
tympanum, -i, n.	drum

U

ubi	where, when
ubinam	where in the world
ulciscor, ulcisci, ultus sum	to take revenge
ulcus, ulceris, n.	sore, ulcer
ullus, -a, -um	any
ulpicum, -i, n.	a variety of garlic
umquam	at any time, ever
una	together, at the same time
unde	from where; from which source
unus, -a, -um	one, single
urbs, urbis, f.	city
urgeo, -ere, ursi	to press down, weigh down upon
uro, -ere, ussi, ustum	to burn
usquam	anywhere
usque	continually; all the way
usus, -us, m.	need, requirement
ut, uti	(w. subjunctive verb) so that, in order that; (w. indicative verb) as, when; how
uter, utra, utrum	which of the two?; whichever of the two
uti	see *ut*
utinam	how I wish that, if only, would that
uxor, uxoris, f.	wife

V

vae	(exclamation of anguish)
vah	(exclamation of surprise, pain, contempt)
valeo, -ere, valui, valitum	to be well; (*vale*) Goodbye!
vapulo, -are	to get a beating, be beaten
vasum, -i, n.	container for liquids
vel	or
venator, venatoris, m.	hunter
vendo, -ere, vendidi, venditum	to sell
veneo, venire, venii, venitum	to be sold
veneror, venerari, veneratus sum	to worship
venio, -ire, veni, ventum	to come
Venus, Veneris, f.	Venus, the goddess of love and passion

venustas, venustatis, f.	charm, grace
venustus, -a, -um	attractive in appearance or manner
verbero, -are	to beat, strike repeatedly
verberetillus, -a, -um	beaten
verbum, -i, n.	word
vero	in fact, really; indeed
versor, -ari	to come and go often, pass one's time
verto, -ere, verti, versum	to turn, change
verum	but
verus, -a, -um	true
vester, vestra, vestrum	your, yours (plural)
vetus, veteris	old; old person
vetustas, vetustatis, f.	old age
via, -ae, f.	road
vicinus, -a, -um	neighboring
victoria, -ae, f.	victory
video, -ere, vidi, visum	to see; to see to, attend to; (passive) to seem
vilica, -ae, f.	female farm overseer
vinco, -ere, vici, victum	to beat, defeat, conquer
vinum, -i, n.	wine
vir, viri, m.	man
virtus, virtutis, f.	virtue
viscum, -i, n.	a sticky paste made from mistletoe berries
viso, -ere, visi	to go and see
vita, -ae, f.	life
vitium, -ii, n.	fault, defect
vivo, -ere, vixi, victum	to live
vix	hardly, with difficulty, barely
voco, -are	to call, invite
volaticus, -a, -um	flying
volo, -are	to fly
volo, velle, volui	to wish
volucer, volucris, volucre	flying
volup	pleasurably; (*volup est mihi*) I'm pleased
voluptarius, -a, -um	characterized by sensual pleasure
voluptas, voluptatis, f.	pleasure
vorsor, -ari	see *versor*
vos	you (plural)
vosmet	-*met* simply intensifies the pronoun *vos*
voster, vostra, vostrum	see *vester*
voto, are, votui, votitum	to forbid
Vt	see *ut*

A Handbook of
Latin Literature
From the earliest
times to the death of
St. Augustine

H. J. Rose

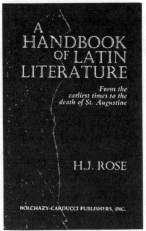

582 pp. (1936, rpt. 1996)
ISBN: 0-86516-317-0
Paperback, $19.00

This reference work offers a matchless over-
view of Latin literature from the beginnings to
the era of St. Augustine. First published in
1936, this book is a penetrating study of Latin
literature and includes not only the classical
and post-classical authors, but also a represen-
tative selection of Christian writers. Each
known work is discussed and analyzed in
terms of content, chronology, genre, significance, meaning, genetic relationship to other
works, ancient and modern scholarship and
influence. Also included is a supplementary
bibliography by E. Courtney.

BOLCHAZY-CARDUCCI Publishers, Inc.

*Music hath charms to soothe the
    savage breast,*

*To soften rocks, or bend a knotted
    oak.*

*I've read that things inanimate have
    moved,*

*And, as with living souls, have been
    inform'd*

*By magic numbers and persuasive
    sound.*

The Mourning Bride, Act I

---

*Sine musica nulla disciplina
potest esse perfecta;
nihil enim est sine illa.*

Latin Music Through the Ages

text by Cynthia Kaldis
choral performance by the Lafayette Chamber Singers
directed by Clayton Lein

Latin Music Through the Ages presents a unique selection of
Latin choral music spanning the medieval, Renaissance and
modern periods. The listener will experience the timeless beauty
of Latin in a wide variety of musical settings, with interpretive
notes on the lyrics, the composers and the story of Latin's
evolution beyond the classical period. The text, by long time
high school Latin teacher, Cynthia Kaldis, accompanies the
recorded performance of the Lafayette Chamber Singers, directed
by Clayton Lein. **Songs include:** ✦ *The Virgin's Cradle
Hymn* ✦ *Song of the Nuns of Chester* ✦ *Orientis Partibus* ✦
Mirabile Mysterium ✦ *O Admirabile Commercium* ✦ *Ubi
Caritas.* **Composers:** e.g. Casals, Arne, Handl, Messaien,
Poulenc, Hildegard, Dufay, et al.

Cassette features choral performance of 17 Latin songs.
ISBN 0-86516-249-2

Book with lyrics, English translations, vocabulary;
composer biographies, background on social/historical
significance of each song, and illustrations.
ISBN 0-86516-242-5

BOLCHAZY-CARDUCCI Publishers, Inc.

LATINE CANTEMUS:
CANTICA POPULARIA LATINE REDDITA

Franz Schlosser
trans. and illus.

112 songs in Latin
40 illustrations
144 pages

This illustrated edition features 64 of Schlosser's new Latin translations of popular songs including:

- **Nursery rhymes** - **Chanties** - **Folk songs**
- **Christmas carols** - **Spirituals**

Also includes three appendices (58 songs) of
- **traditional Latin favorites**
- **Christmas songs**
- **well-known Gregorian chants.**

"... an amazing variety of songs, old and new, from many cultures ... a good resource for the classroom and Latin club."
JoAnn Sweeney, Loyola University, Chicago [Emerita]

"This attractive collection of songs and hymns will delight novice Latinists and experts alike both within and outside the classroom. It makes a great gift for persons of all ages with any Latin in their background."
Dr. Rudolph Masciantonio
Director of Foreign Language Education Emeritus
The School District of Philadelphia

illu., viii + 135 p. (1996), Paperback, ISBN: 0-86516-315-4

BOLCHAZY-CARDUCCI Publishers, Inc.

Baroque Music from the Bolivian Rainforest
conducted by Piotr Nawrot
performed by the Cathedral Singers and
the Symphony of the Shores Chamber Players.

CD with dual-language libretto. Once heard only at
Vespers in the 17th-century Jesuit Reductions of Bolivia,
this fusion of baroque and native rhythms and melodies is
again brought to life in this stirring performance.

Order #BB10

The Legend Lives Forever in Latin
sung by Jukka Ammondt

ELVIS songs IN LATIN on CD with dual-language
libretto. In a twist unique to our times, this collection of
golden oldies — sung in an even older language — has
become one of Europe's hottest-selling CDs. The disk
features such songs as *Tenere Me Ama* ("Love Me Tender"),
Nunc Aeternitatis ("Surrender"), *Non Adamare Non Possum*
("Can't Help Falling in Love"), and of course, *Impossibile*
("It's Impossible").

Order #62002

BOLCHAZY-CARDUCCI Publishers, Inc.

CARMINA BURANA

BY
JUDITH LYNN SEBESTA

WITH ITS PROVOCATIVE SUBJECT MATTER AND EVOCATIVE MUSIC *CARMINA BURANA* MAKES LATIN A VIBRANT, LIVING LANGUAGE.

ORIGINAL LATIN POEMS, FACING VOCABULARY, ESSAYS

ENGLISH TRANSLATION BY **JEFFERY M. DUBAN**

FEATURING MEDIEVAL WOODCUTS AS WELL AS 17 ORIGINAL ILLUSTRATIONS BY **THOM KAPHEIM.**

Carl Orff's 24 selections from 200 poems of the *Carmina Burana* celebrate the universal range of human emotion and experience: passion, longing, exuberance, humor, rebellion, ennui, resignation. Now tender, now tragic; secular yet reverent; the poems of the Carmina touch the chords of our purest and darkest spirituality.

An excellent resource for the student, the performer, the audience and the general reader, this dual language edition provides two moving translations of the original Latin, facing vocabulary, and informative essays. This text will enrich understanding and heighten appreciation of these beloved medieval poems.

A must for anyone interested in performing Carmina Burana. An engaging book for both singers and conductors. Literal and poetic translations and plentiful period illustrations fascinate and entertain the reader.
    — **Vance George,** Director, San Francisco Symphony Chorus

A delightful and educational supplement for your daily Latin fare...Sebesta's commentary keeps the music constantly in the mind.
                    — **Peter L. Reid,** NEC Newsletter

illu., 164 p. (1985, 2nd ed. 1996) Paperback, ISBN: 0-86516-268-9

BOLCHAZY-CARDUCCI Publishers, Inc.

SING CATULLUS & HORACE

♩

Schola Cantans
composed by Jan Novák

♫

A **cassette** with musical arrangement of
Catullus (34) Dianae Sumus in Fide
Catullus (5) Vivamus Mea Lesbia
♫ *Catullus* (61) Collis O Heliconii
Horace (Carm. 1, 22) Integer Vitae
Horace (Carm. 1,2) Iam Satis Terris
Horace (epod. 15) Nox Erat
(Anonym.) Gaudeamus Igitur
Anth. Lat. (388) Nautarum Carmen
Caesar (BG 1, 1-3) Gallia Est Omnis Divisa
Carmina Burana (142) Tempus Adest Floridum
Carmina Burana (85) Veris Dulcis in Tempore
Martial (10, 62) Ludi Magister
Phaedrus (1,13) Vulpis et Corvus

♩

Cassette: | *Libretto with Score:*
ISBN 0-86516-357-X | ISBN 0-86516-358-8

BOLCHAZY-CARDUCCI Publishers, Inc.

2003. 12. 22   22,50